Annabel Karmel's
FAMILY MEAL PLANNER

Annabel Karmel's
FAMILY MEAL PLANNER

Over 150 wonderfully easy and healthy recipes for all the family

from the best-selling author of

THE NEW COMPLETE BABY & TODDLER MEAL PLANNER

EBURY PRESS
LONDON

**For my children Nicholas, Lara and Scarlett
a constant source of inspiration**

First published in 1999

1 3 5 7 9 10 8 6 4 2

First published in the United Kingdom in 1999 by Ebury Press
Random House, 20 Vauxhall Bridge Road, London SW1V 2SA

Random House Australia (Pty) Limited
20 Alfred Street, Milsons Point, Sydney,
New South Wales 2061, Australia

Random House New Zealand Limited
18 Poland Road, Glenfield, Auckland 10, New Zealand

Random House South Africa (Pty) Limited
Endulini, 5a Jubilee Road, Parktown 2193, South Africa

Random House UK Limited Red. No. 954009

A CIP catalogue record for this book is available from the British Library.

ISBN 0 09 186795 9

Project editor Emma Callery
Designer Alison Shackleton
Photographs Daniel Pangbourne,
except for the pictures on page 7 by Harry Ormisher and page 49 by Philip Wilkins
Home economist Val Barrett
Stylist Tessa Evelegh
Illustrations Nadine Wickenden
Consultant nutritionist Christine Carter Bsc SRD Specialist Paediatric Dietitian at Great Ormond Street Hospital for Sick Children

Printed and bound in Italy by New Interlitho Italia S.p.a., Milan

Contents

Introduction **6**

Breakfast suggestions **26**

Soups, snacks and lunchboxes **40**

Pasta **62**

Poultry **78**

Meat **96**

Fish **110**

Vegetarian dishes **130**

Cakes and biscuits **152**

Desserts **176**

Index **188**

Acknowledgements **191**

Introduction

This book will take the worry out of every-day cooking because with it alongside you, you will know that you'll always have something in the house that can be made into a tasty meal for the family. There are tried and tested recipes for all occasions from healthy breakfasts, through to lunchboxes, family suppers, recipes for entertaining and even fun foods for children to cook themselves. As a busy mother of three children, I know how difficult it can be to find the time to make a home-cooked meal and so I have tried to create recipes that are quick and easy to prepare, healthy and, of course, tasty. Each recipe has been tested on a panel of children who, naturally, didn't care how healthy the food was and were only impressed if it tasted good.

For many children, convenience and junk foods are no longer occasional foods but are becoming a regular part of their diet and in this age of instant gratification, fewer and fewer families are sitting down to meals togeth-er. With the proliferation of processed pack-aged foods, many meals emanate from the freezer to be cooked in the microwave and the kitchen is fast becoming the coldest room in the house. Healthy eating for children is crucial as

it often sets the dietary pattern for life, and eat-ing healthily from a young age can reduce the risk of developing diet-related diseases like heart disease and some forms of cancer. For fighting disease, food is still the best medicine.

Food is more than just a biological need, its preparation expresses parental love and caring and it's so very satisfying to see your family enjoy your lovingly prepared home-cooked meals. There was once a time when children ate largely the same as their parents and this book aims to provide you with recipes that the whole family will enjoy together. You don't need to be a Supercook. These recipes don't require split-second timing, special skills or expensive equipment and most of them can be prepared in less than 30 minutes.

Some weeks you'll be able to plan ahead and know what you're going to feed the family for supper on Friday when it's still only Monday, and other weeks you may only have time to think about Friday's dinner on Friday.

A bit of time spent planning, cooking ahead and freezing some meals over the weekend will make the week ahead much more manageable. Decide on the week's meals and what advance cooking you can do over the weekend. Then make a shopping list for the week and jot down on a calendar the fresh ingredients you will need to pick up during the week. Naturally there will be weekends where you're busy or the weather is too nice to spend time in the kitchen and so you can just plan simple meals for the week ahead like Teriyaki Chicken Skewers (page 81), Salad and Fresh Fruit. There will also be occasions when you haven't even had time to do the shopping and it's already six o'clock, but you don't need to panic as there are lots of ideas here for delicious recipes which can be made from basic store-cupboard ingredients.

Rather than thinking what are we going to eat and what are the children going to eat, we should be thinking of one meal for the whole family. A good solution to the problem of family members who want meals at different times of the day is to freeze some food in individual portion sizes so that you have your own stock of healthy convenience foods that can be heated up in the microwave in a matter of minutes. Very often when you are making a recipe it takes very little extra time to prepare more than you need so you have portions leftover to freeze.

International cuisine can be another source of inspiration – perhaps make a Chinese dinner for the family choosing some of the delicious easy to prepare Chinese-style recipes from the book such as Super vegetarian spring rolls followed by Chinese noodles with prawns and beansprouts and lychees with Caramelised almond ice cream for dessert. Wouldn't it be fun to eat the food with chopsticks – you can buy child friendly-plastic chopsticks that are joined at the top, which makes it very easy for children to use them.

This is a book of everyday family eating and I hope it will be well-thumbed and splattered with food and will help busy lifestyles become less chaotic. My aim is that this book will put the joy back into cooking, which is after all a labour of love.

Annabel Karmel

Organization

It's getting late, you've got work to finish for the next day, the phone keeps ringing, the children want help with their homework and you haven't even thought about what you can make for supper. Do you find yourself staring at the contents of your larder for inspiration – well, here's the answer to your problems.

First of all a list of ingredients to stock in your kitchen so that you will always be able to rustle up a delicious meal for the family and secondly lots of recipes which can be frozen ahead. It takes very little extra effort or time to cook more than you need and freeze extra portions so you always have a store of tasty, healthy recipes which can be defrosted and cooked at your convenience.

Coming up with varied meals can't always be done at the last minute and so you will need to spend a bit of time planning ahead. The Menu Planners have been designed to help you plan your cooking and shopping each week (see pages 10-17).

Don't feel you have to stick to these. It's perfectly OK to substitute simple meals like omelettes, bought pizzas and fish fingers for some of the meals so there is a combination of ready-prepared and freshly cooked food. Also, a cold snack for toddlers, such as a cheese and salad sandwich, can be as nutritious as a hot meal.

THE HEALTHY STORECUPBOARD

The key to making your life easier when it comes to planning weekly menus is stocking your kitchen with good basic ingredients. I have put together lists of the foods you need to try to keep in stock, basing them on the recipes in the book. Don't feel that you have to buy everything at once and you could simply choose a selection of recipes that you would like to prepare and just buy the ingredients for those recipes.

Dry foods
Bread
Rice: eg white and brown long-grain rice
Flour: wholemeal plain, self-raising, cornflour, strong white
Baking soda
Bicarbonate of soda
Dried yeast
Pasta: penne, tagliatelle, spaghettini, short-cut macaroni, lasagne, Chinese egg noodles
Sugar: caster sugar, light brown sugar, light muscovado sugar, icing sugar
Breakfast cereal: porridge, muesli, wheatgerm, etc.
Dried fruit: eg apricots, raisins, sultanas
Nuts: ground almonds, pecans, peanuts
Grains that don't take long to prepare, eg couscous, bulgar wheat
Split red lentils, green lentils
Desiccated coconut
Good quality plain chocolate
Cocoa powder
Skimmed milk powder

Tinned produce and jars
Chopped plum tomatoes
Sweetcorn
Baked beans
Red kidney beans
Good quality ready-made tomato sauce
Sun-dried tomatoes
Peanut butter
Golden syrup, maple syrup, honey
Yeast extract
Sardines
Tuna fish in oil
Condensed cream of tomato soup
Condensed cream of mushroom soup
Condensed milk
Evaporated milk
Mandarin oranges
Raspberries
Peaches

Dried herbs and ground spices
Mixed dried herbs, basil, bay leaves, oregano, thyme, marjoram, paprika, turmeric, cumin, chilli powder, blades of mace, nutmeg, black peppercorns, cinnamon, curry powder, ground ginger

Fruit and vegetables
Variety of fruit
Salad vegetables
Onions

Garlic
Fresh ginger

Sauces, oils and seasonings
Olive oil, sunflower oil, vegetable oil,
sesame oil
Red wine vinegar, balsamic vinegar, rice
wine vinegar (may find in Oriental food
section of store), cider vinegar, malt
vinegar
Soy sauce
Oyster sauce
Worcestershire sauce
Tomato purée
Tomato sauce
Red pesto
Hoisin sauce
Salad cream
Mayonnaise
Honey
Maple syrup
Curry powder
Dry mustard powder
Dijon mustard
Chicken stock and vegetable stock
cubes or use jars of stock
Sesame seeds
Pure vanilla essence
Lemon juice

Alcohol
Dry white wine
Sake
Mirin
Sherry

IN THE REFRIGERATOR

To obtain the longest life possible
from perishable foods it would be a
good idea to wash and tidy your
fridge once a week.

Check its temperature: it should be
32-41°F (0-5°C) and if your fridge
is not already equipped with a
thermometer, it would be a good
idea to purchase one – many
fridges do not store food at a low
enough temperature.

Dairy and cooked foods should be
stored at the top of the fridge with
raw meats below in a sealed
container.

Butter
Soft margarine
Low-fat plain yoghurt
Cheddar cheese
Gruyère cheese
Edam cheese
Parmesan cheese
Cream cheese
Eggs
Milk
Ready-made custard

IN THE FREEZER

It's a good idea to freeze bread and
butter for emergencies. It's also
good to keep some ready-made
frozen foods like pizzas, or chicken
or fish in breadcrumbs in the
freezer.

Frozen peas
Frozen leaf spinach
Frozen sweetcorn
Frozen low-fat oven chips
Frozen pizza
Frozen chicken breasts
Fish fillets with or without
breadcrumbs
Lean minced meat
Lamb chops
Good quality dairy ice cream
Frozen raspberries

If you are buying fish or chicken
in breadcrumbs or batter, choose
larger portion sizes as there will be
less coating in proportion to the
fish or chicken.

Buy thick-cut oven chips – the
thicker they are, the lesss fat they
contain.

TIP
Keep a shopping list in the kitchen and have a house rule that whoever uses up the last of
something adds the item to the list.

SPRING MEAL PLANNER

	BREAKFAST	LUNCH	DINNER	LUNCHBOX RECIPES
DAY 1	Apple and carrot breakfast muffins* (p36) Fruit salad with honey yoghurt dressing (p29)	Ratatouille omelette (p146) Fruit	Marinated of beef with vegetables (p104) Nicholas's dream dessert (p186)	Apple and carrot breakfast muffins (p36) Annabel's tasty chicken skewers (p81) Delicious vegetable rissoles (p146)
DAY 2	Boiled or scrambled egg with toast Yoghurt Fruit	Three-cheese macaroni* (p68) Salad Forest fruit lollies (p176) or fruit	Annabel's tasty chicken skewers (p81) Courgette fritters (p138) Berried treasure (p186)	Ratatouille omelette (p146) Coconut kisses (p165) Annabel's apricot cookies (p160)
DAY 3	Cereal Stewed fruit Fromage frais	Quick ciabatta pizza (p51) Salad Fruit	Soupa tuna tagliatelle* (p127) Salad Tiramisu (p181)	**KIDS IN THE KITCHEN RECIPES**
DAY 4	Welsh rarebit (p34) Yoghurt Fruit	Delicious vegetable rissoles* (p146) Mozzarella and tomato salad Ice cream and fruit	Creamy chicken with vegetables* (p84) Mashed potato with carrot (p142) Very easy raspberry mousse (p177)	Three-cheese macaroni (p68) Quick ciabatta pizza (p51) Soupa tuna tagliatelle (p127)
DAY 5	Fruity homemade muesli (p38) Cheese Fruit	Linguine with spring vegetables (p70) Salad Orange jelly with mandarins	Marinated beef skewers (p106) Perfect Chinese fried rice (p132) Coconut kisses* (p165)	Annabel's tasty chicken skewers (p81) Lemon and raisin drop scones (p38)
DAY 6	French toast (p35) Fromage frais Fruit	Evelyn's tasty fish pie* (p126) Vegetables Annabel's apricot cookies* (p160)	Orient Express (p66) Auntie Ruthie's quick and easy cheesecake* (p180) Fruit	Nicholas's dream dessert (p186) Very easy raspberry mousse (p177) Annabel's apricot cookies (p160)
DAY 7	Lemon and raisin drop scones* (p38) Cereal Fruit	Tagliatelle with prawns and vegetables* (p75) Desert island pineapple (p178)	Turkey meatballs with tomato sauce* (p85) Rice and Gratin of courgette (p138) Fruit	Coconut kisses (p165) Auntie Ruthie's quick and easy cheesecake (p180) Tiramisu (p181)

* = freeze-ahead recipes

SHOPPING LIST

In addition to a well-stocked store cupboard (see pages 8-9) you will need to buy the following ingredients

DAY 1
Dairy produce: 300 ml (½ pint) whipping cream, 75 ml (3 fl oz) double cream, 4 ready-made meringues, 100 g (4 oz) Gruyère cheese
Fresh produce: 1 apple, 175 g (7 oz) carrots, 100 g (4 oz) French beans, 75 g (6 oz) new potatoes, 2 red peppers, 1 aubergine, 1 large courgette, 2 tomatoes, 450 g (1 lb) raspberries (fresh or frozen), 175 g (6 oz) strawberries
Meat: 225 g (8 oz) fillet or rump steak

DAY 2
Dairy produce: 50 g (2 oz) Gruyère cheese, 1 X 150 g (5 oz) pot raspberry yoghurt
Fresh produce: 2 peaches, 6 plums or apricots, 150 g (6 oz) each raspberries, strawberries, blackberries, blueberries, 100 g (4 oz) cherries, 450 g (1 lb) courgettes
Poultry: 4 chicken breasts

DAY 3
Dairy produce: 400 g (14 oz) Mascarpone cheese
Fresh produce: 450 g (1 lb) cooking apples or rhubarb, 2 button mushrooms, 2 tomatoes, 3 tbsp fresh basil, 1 tsp snipped chives
Meat: 40 g (1½ oz) pepperoni
Additonal 4 tbsp Marsala wine, 24 boudoir biscuits, 1 small ciabatta loaf

DAY 4
Dairy produce: 1 packet Mozzarella cheese, 3 to 4 tbsp double cream
Fresh produce: 500 g (1 lb 2 oz) tomatoes, 500 g (1 lb 2 oz) potatoes, 75 g (3 oz) baby carrots, 3 large carrots 100 g (4 oz) butternut squash, 1 leek, 75 g (3 oz) French beans, 3 shallots, 225 g (8 oz) button mushrooms, 1 tbsp parsley, 1 lemon
Poultry: 4 chicken breasts
Additonal 1 X 400 g (14 oz) can of raspberries, 1 X 135 g (4½ oz) packet raspberry jelly, 50 ml (2 fl oz) white wine

DAY 5
Fresh produce: 4 tomatoes, 350 g (12 oz) carrots, 2 red peppers, 2 spring onions, 4 button mushrooms
Meat: 350 g (12 oz) fillet steak
350 ml (12 fl oz) apple and mango or apple juice, 1 X 135 g (4½ oz) orange jelly, 1 tin mandarin segments

DAY 6
Dairy produce: 600 ml (1 pint) sour cream, 100 g (4 oz) cream cheese
Fresh produce: 1 large red pepper, 1 small green pepper, 1 tbsp parsley, 100 g (4 oz) broccoli, 100 g (4 oz) baby corn, 100 g (4 oz) carrots, 75 g (3 oz) button mushrooms, 2 tbsp sliced spring onion, 550 g (1¼ lb) strawberries
Poultry: 2 chicken breasts
Additonal 225 g (8 oz) digestive biscuits, 65 g (2½ oz) white chocolate chips or white chocolate, seedless raspberry jam

DAY 7
Dairy produce:: 200 ml (7 fl oz) crème fraîche or light crème fraîche
Fresh produce: 2 apples, 175 g (6 oz) cauliflower, 1 medium carrot, 50 g (2 oz) French beans, 100 g (4 oz) small courgettes, bunch fresh parsley, 100 g (4 oz) leek, 1 tbsp fresh thyme, 500 g (1 lb 2 oz) courgettes, 1 large pineapple, bunch of white grapes, 225 g (8 oz) strawberries
Poultry: 450 g (1 lb) minced turkey
Fish: 175 g (6 oz) cooked king prawns (fresh or frozen)

SUMMER MEAL PLANNER

	BREAKFAST	LUNCH	DINNER	LUNCHBOX RECIPES
DAY 1	Fruity homemade muesli (p38) Yoghurt Fruit	Annabel's 15-minute tomato sauce* (p64) and spaghetti Salad Fruit	Chicken balls in sweet and sour sauce* (p80) Rice and vegetables Berried treasure (p186)	Easy yakitori chicken (p94) Turkey burgers (p86) Dressing for dinner with pasta salad (p55) Apple and carrot breakfast muffins (p36)
DAY 2	Boiled or scrambled egg and toast Yoghurt Fruit	Fluffy baked potatoes (p136) Salad and Dressing for dinner sauce (p55) Forest fruit lollies (p178) or fruit	Crudités and dip Simply super salmon teriyaki (p118) and rice Summer fruit brulée with amaretto (p176)	Berried treasure (p186) Fruit salad with honey yoghurt dressing (p29)
DAY 3	Cereal Cheese Fruit salad with honey yoghurt dressing (p29)	Vegetable tagliatelle* (p74) Tomato salad Fruit	Annabel's tasty chicken skewers (p81) Perfect Chinese fried rice (p132) Caramelised almond ice cream (p176) and fruit	
DAY 4	Apple and carrot breakfast muffins* (p36) Cereal Fruity milkshake (p29)	Yummy fish in orange sauce (p116) Salad Fruit	Mini meatballs with tomato sauce* (p98) with tagliatelle Apple and plum crumble* (p184) with custard	**KIDS IN THE KITCHEN RECIPES**
DAY 5	Breakfast sundae (p29) French toast (p35)	Easy yakitori chicken (p94) Gratin of carrots with a crunchy topping* (p141) Fruit	Perfect paella* (p123) Salad Tiramisu (p179)	Scrambled eggs (p29) Dressing for dinner (p35) Apple and carrot breakfast muffins (p36) Gratin of carrots with crunchy topping (p141)
DAY 6	Perfect pancakes (p35) Yoghurt Fruit	Turkey burgers* (p86) and oven-baked chips Broccoli and carrots Nicholas's dream dessert (p186)	Summer risotto (p134) Salad Frozen yoghurt ice cream (p185) and fruit	Perfect pancakes (p35) Forest fruit lollies (p178) Summer fruit brulée with amaretto (p176) Caramelised almond ice cream (p176) Apple and plum crumble (p184) Frozen yoghurt ice cream (p185)
DAY 7	Boiled or scrambled egg and toast Fruit	Summer barbecue of Heavenly barbecued burgers (p86), Teriyaki chicken skewers (p81), Corn on the cob, Baked potatoes (p135), Salad Desert island pineapple (p178)	Tagliatelle with prawns and vegetables* (p75) Fruit and ice cream	

* = freeze-ahead recipes

12

SHOPPING LIST

In addition to a well-stocked store cupboard (see pages 8-9) you will need to buy the following ingredients

DAY 1

Fresh produce: 1 small red pepper, 1 tbsp each fresh basil and parsley, 100 g (4 oz) each strawberries, blackberries, blueberries, cherries, raspberries, 2 ripe peaches, 6 plums or apricots, 2 apples

Poultry: 2 chicken breasts

Additonal 350 ml (12 fl oz) apple and mango or apple juice, 150 ml (5 fl oz) pineapple juice

DAY 2

Dairy produce: 1 X 150 g (5 oz) pot raspberry yoghurt, 300 ml (½ pint) crème fraîche, ready-made dip, eg cream cheese and chive

Fresh produce: 150 g (5 oz) mushrooms, 150 g (5 oz) beansprouts, 2 baking potatoes, raw vegetables for crudités, 1 bunch celery, 200 g (7 oz) raspberries, 200 g (7 oz) blueberries, 50 g (2 oz) strawberries, 50 g (2 oz) blackberries, 2 ripe peaches, 1 lemon

Fish: 4 X 150 g (5 oz) fillets of salmon, skinned

Additonal 50 g (2 oz) amaretto biscuits

DAY 3

Dairy produce: 100 ml (4 oz) light crème fraîche, 300 ml (½ pint) double cream

Fresh produce: 50 g (2 oz) carrots, 1 small yellow pepper, 450 g (1 lb) tomatoes, 1 medium courgette, 8 cherry tomatoes, ½ baby gem lettuce, 1 lemon, 1 spring onion

Poultry: 4 chicken breasts

Additonal 225 g (8 oz) blanched almonds

DAY 4

Fresh produce: 225 g (8 oz) carrots, 4 tomatoes, 175 g (6 oz) courgettes, 100 g (4 oz) red pepper, 1 tbsp fresh parsley, 2 apples, 1 orange, 4 ripe plums, 1 kg (2 1b) cooking apples

Fish: 225 g (8 oz) fillet of cod, haddock or hake

Meat: 450 g (1 lb) lean minced beef

DAY 5

Dairy produce: 75 g (3 oz) Gruyère cheese, 400 g (14 oz) Mascarpone cheese

Fresh produce 2 spring onions, 450 g (1 lb) carrots, 1 red pepper, 3 tbsp fresh parsley,

Poultry: 2 chicken breasts

Fish: 150 g (5 oz) fresh prawns, 225 g (8 oz) fresh clams, 350 g (12 oz) fresh mussels

Additonal 24 boudoir biscuits

DAY 6

Dairy produce: 720 ml (1¼ pint) whipping cream

Fresh produce: 225 g (8 oz) broccoli, 2 carrots, 1 red pepper, 125 g (4½ oz) courgettes, 2 tomatoes, 1 tbsp fresh thyme or oregano, 1 apple, 450 g (1 lb) raspberries, 175 g (6 oz) strawberries

Poultry: 450 g (1 lb) minced turkey   *Additonal:* 125 ml (4 fl oz) white wine, 4 ready-made meringues

DAY 7

Dairy produce: 4 tbsp light crème fraîche

Fresh produce: 1½ red peppers, 3 tbsp parsley, 4 corn on the cob, 4 baking potatoes, 175 g (6 oz) cauliflower, 1 medium carrot, 50 g (2 oz) French beans, 100 g (4 oz) small courgettes, 1 apple, 1 lime/lemon, 50 g (2 oz) button mushrooms

Poultry: 4 chicken breasts   *Meat:* 450 g (1 lb) minced beef, 350 g (12 oz) fillet steak   *Fish:* 175 g (6 oz) cooked king prawns

AUTUMN MEAL PLANNER

	BREAKFAST	LUNCH	DINNER	LUNCHBOX RECIPES
DAY 1	Welsh rarebit (p34) Yoghurt and honey Fruit	Lara's lovely onion soup* (p44) Brown rice 'risotto' (p148) Fruit	Chicken piccata* (p84) and spinach Mashed potato with carrot (p142) Yvonne's malva pudding (p185)	Apple and carrot breakfast muffins (p36) Caramelised onion and gruyère tart (p142) Easy yakitori chicken (p94)
DAY 2	Boiled or poached egg Toast Dried fruit compote (p29) or prunes	Scarlett's pasta (p76) Salad Fruit	Tasty 10-minute prawn stir-fry (p112) Perfect Chinese fried rice (p132) Fruit and ice cream	Mummy's Minestrone (p46) Mediterranean tomato soup (p49)
DAY 3	Cereal or porridge Yoghurt Fruit	Caramelised onion and gruyère tart* (p142) Salad Fruit	Mini meatballs with tomato sauce* (p98) Rice Tiramisu (p179) or fruit	**KIDS IN THE KITCHEN RECIPES**
DAY 4	Apple and carrot breakfast muffins* (p36) Cereal Fruit	Teriyaki glazed mackerel fillets (p113) Vegetables Fruit	Lasagne with spinach, cheese and tomato* (p69) Louise's apple and blackberry pudding (p177) with custard	Spaghetti bolognese (p68) Annabel's 15-minute tomato sauce (p64)
DAY 5	Scrambled eggs Toast Stewed apple	Annabel's 15-minute tomato sauce* (p64) and spaghetti Salad Fruit	Mummy's minestrone* (p46) Easy yakitori chicken (p94) Yummy vegetables in oyster sauce (p148) Fruit	Yvonne's malva pudding (p185) Tiramisu (p179) Louise's apple and blackberry pudding (p177) Apple and plum crumble (p184)
DAY 6	Savoury breakfast muffins (p36) Cereal Fruit	Honeyed lamb cutlets (p102) Baked potatoes (p136) Broccoli and carrots Fruit	Mediterranean tomato soup* (p49) Penne with chicken, tomatoes and basil (p73) Apple and plum crumble* (p184) with custard	
DAY 7	French toast (p35) Yoghurt and honey Fruit	Spaghetti bolognese* (p68) Baked marrow with a cheesy topping (p132) Fruit	Fruity curried chicken* (p88) Rice Evelyn's lokshen pudding (p184)	

* = freeze-ahead recipes

SHOPPING LIST

In addition to a well-stocked store cupboard (see pages 8-9) you will need to buy the following ingredients

DAY 1

Dairy produce: 75 g (3 oz) Gruyère cheese, 250 ml (8 fl oz) whipping or double cream

Fresh produce: 675 g (1½ lb) potatoes, 2 large carrots, 100 g (4 oz) broccoli, 100 g (4 oz) cauliflower, 100 g (4 oz) courgette, 1 spring onion, 1 lemon

Poultry: 2 chicken breasts

150 ml (5 fl oz) white wine, 1 small French loaf, apricot jam

DAY 2

Fresh produce: 2 shallots, ½ small red pepper, 100 g (4 oz) baby sweetcorn, 150 g (5 oz) carrots, 1 tbsp basil, 2 spring onions, 100 g (4 oz) sugar snap peas or mangetout

Meat: 100 g (4 oz) salami

Fish: 225 g (8 oz) cooked king prawns

Additional: 1 packet mixed dried fruit or 2 tins prunes

DAY 3

Dairy produce: 150 g (5 oz) Gruyère cheese, 300 ml (½ pint) cream

Fresh produce: 175 g (6 oz) carrots, 175 g (6 oz) courgettes, 100 g (4 oz) red pepper, 1 tbsp parsley

Additional: 4 tbsp Marsala wine

DAY 4

Dairy produce: 175 g (6 oz) cottage cheese, 125 g (4½ oz) Mozzarella cheese, 2 tbsp double cream

Fresh produce: 1 apple, 75 g (3 oz) carrots, 100 g (4 oz) button mushrooms, 225 g (8 oz) beansprouts, 450 g (1 lb) fresh or 225 g (8 oz) frozen spinach, 1 tbsp each basil and parsley, 450 g (1 lb) cooking apples, 225 g (8 oz) blackberries (fresh or frozen)

Additional: 100 g (4 oz) ground almonds

DAY 5

Fresh produce: 2 cooking apples, 1 small red chilli, 1 tbsp fresh basil, 1 leek, 225 g (8 oz) carrots, 100 g (4 oz) potatoes, 100 g (4 oz) French beans, 50 g (2 oz) celery, 2 spring onions, 100 g (4 oz) broccoli, 100 g (4 oz) baby sweetcorn, 75 g (3 oz) mushrooms

Poultry: 2 chicken breasts

DAY 6

Dairy produce: 150 ml (5 fl oz) crème fraîche

Fresh produce: 450 g (1 lb) carrots, 2 sticks celery, 2 baking potatoes, 1½ tbsp fresh tarragon, 3 tbsp basil, 295 g (10 oz) broccoli, 500 g (1 lb 2 oz) plum tomatoes, 2 shallots, 1 kg (2 lb) cooking apples, 4 ripe plums

Poultry: 2 chicken breasts

Meat: 6 lamb cutlets

Additional: 25 g (1 oz) pine kernels, 50 g (2 oz) sun-dried tomatoes

DAY 7

Dairy produce: 3 tbsp double cream

Fresh produce: 100 g (4 oz) button mushrooms, 1 medium-sized marrow, 1 tbsp each parsley and basil, 1 large carrot, 1 lemon, 1 cooking apple

Poultry: 1 large chicken

Meat: 500 g (1 lb 2 oz) minced beef or lamb

WINTER MEAL PLANNER

	BREAKFAST	LUNCH	DINNER	LUNCHBOX RECIPES
DAY 1	Swirly porridge (p30) Yoghurt Fruit	Mediterranean tomato soup* (p49) Fluffy baked potatoes (p136) Fruit	Simon's multi-layered shepherd's pie (p108) Rhubarb crumble* (p184) with custard	Mediterranean tomato soup (p49) Nourishing lentil soup (p45) Mummy's minestrone (p46) Tasty and healthy vegetable soup (p45) Potato, leek and watercress soup (p46) Vegetable burgers (p143)
DAY 2	Cereal Cheese on toast Fruit	Vegetable burgers* (p143) Baked beans Fruit	Fruity curried chicken* (p88) Rice and poppadums Tiramisu (p179)	
DAY 3	Boiled or scrambled egg Toast Stewed apple	Turkey bolognese* (p74) Salad with Dressing for dinner sauce (p55) Fruit	Mummy's minestrone* (p46) Posh fish fingers (p122) and oven-baked chips Louise's apple and blackberry pudding (p177)	Finger licking chicken drumsticks (p89) Chicken burgers with courgette and apple (p92) Best-ever oatmeal raisin cookies (p169)
DAY 4	Cereal Yoghurt Fruit	Finger licking chicken drumsticks (p89) Mini baked potatoes (p137) Best-ever oatmeal raisin cookies* (p169) and ice cream	Good old-fashioned chicken soup* (p47) Lara's lasagne* (p64) Fruit	**KIDS IN THE KITCHEN RECIPES**
DAY 5	Welsh rarebit (p34) Dried fruit compote (p29) or prunes Fromage frais	Nourishing lentil soup* (p45) Super vegetarian spring rolls* (p140) Fruit	Chicken burgers with courgette and apple* (p92) Brown rice 'risotto' (p148) Raspberry jelly with peaches	
DAY 6	Cheese, chive and tomato omelette (p34) Toast Fruit	Spaghetti bolognese (p68) Salad Chocolate banana pancakes with toffee sauce* (p182)	Potato, leek and watercress soup (p46) Very easy Florentine fillets (p112) Evelyn's lokshen pudding (p184)	Lara's lasagne (p64) Spaghetti bolognese (p68) Mini baked potatoes (p137) Best-ever oatmeal raisin cookies (p169) Tiramisu (p179) Louise's apple and blackberry pudding (p177)
DAY 7	Waffles and maple syrup Yoghurt Fruit	Lloyd's leg of lamb (p103) Roast potatoes and vegetables Apple and plum crumble* (p184) with custard	Tasty and healthy vegetable soup* (p45) Chinese noodles with prawns and beansprouts (p128) Fruit	Apple and plum crumble (p184) Chocolate banana pancakes with toffee sauce (p182)

* = freeze-ahead recipes

SHOPPING LIST

In addition to a well-stocked store cupboard (see pages 8-9) you will need to buy the following ingredients

DAY 1

Fresh produce:	675 g (1 lb 8 oz) carrots, 2 celery sticks, 550 g (1 lb 4 oz) potatoes, 2 baking potatoes, 500 g (1 lb 2 oz) plum tomatoes, 1½ tbsp each basil and tarragon, 1 kg (2 lb) rhubarb
Meat:	450 g (1 lb) minced beef or lamb

DAY 2

Dairy produce:	400 g (14 oz) Mascarpone cheese
Fresh produce:	3 carrots, 1 courgette, 50 g (2 oz) button mushrooms, 1 tbsp each fresh oregano and parsley, 1 cooking apple, 1 lemon
Poultry:	1 roasting chicken
Additional	poppadums, Marsala wine, 24 boudoir biscuits

DAY 3

Fresh produce:	1 potato, 100 g (4 oz) French beans, 1 leek, 1 red pepper, 2 carrots, 2 sticks celery, 1tbsp each parsley, thyme and sage, 1 kg (2 lb) cooking apples, 225 g (8 oz) blackberries (fresh or frozen)
Fish:	450 g (1 lb) cod, haddock or plaice fillets, skinned

DAY 4

Dairy produce:	50 g (2 oz) Gruyère cheese
Fresh produce:	450 g (1 lb) new potatoes, 3 large carrots, 2 parsnips, 1 leek, 1 stick celery, 1 red pepper, 2 sprigs parsley
Poultry:	4 large chicken drumsticks, 1 large boiler chicken plus giblets
Meat:	450 g (1 lb) lean minced beef

DAY 5

Fresh produce:	1 leek, 550 g (1 lb 4 oz) carrots, 50 g (2 oz) celery, 1 potato, 3 tbsp parsley, 100 g (4 oz) baby sweetcorn, 100 g (4 oz) button mushrooms, 50 g (2 oz) red pepper, 225 g (8 oz) Chinese cabbage, bunch of spring onions, 12 courgettes, 100 g (4 oz) broccoli, 100 g (4 oz) cauliflower, 2 apples
Poultry:	2 breasts of chicken
Additional	Spring roll wrappers, tinned prunes or mixed dried fruit, 1 packet raspberry jelly, 1 tin sliced peaches

DAY 6

Dairy produce:	250 ml (8 fl oz) double cream, 100 g (4 oz) Dolcelatte cheese
Fresh produce:	2 tomatoes, 100 g (4 oz) button mushrooms, ½ tbsp snipped chives, 900 g (2 lb) potatoes, 1 leek, 2 X 85 g (3½ oz) bags watercress, 225 g (8 oz) fresh or 100 g (4 oz) frozen spinach, 4 bananas
Meat:	500 g (1 lb 2 oz) lean minced beef
Fish:	225 g (8 oz) fillet of cod or haddock skinned

DAY 7

Fresh produce:	400 g (14 oz) carrots, 1 large potato, 250 g (8½ oz) button mushrooms, 1 celery stalk, 4 spring onions, 1 tbsp parsley, 100 g (4 oz) beansprouts, 1 small red chilli, 1 kg (2 lb) cooking apples, 4 ripe plums
Meat:	1 leg of lamb
Fish:	100 g (4 oz) large cooked peeled prawns
Additional	waffles, 175 g (6 oz) Chinese noodles

The Food Pyramid

Eating a balanced diet is all to do with choosing the right foods and eating them in the right proportion. For most of us that will mean eating more bread, cereals, starchy foods like potatoes, pasta and rice and more fruits and vegetables. This is the type of diet that adults and children over five should be eating.

Children under five need a diet higher in fat and lower in fibre because of their high energy requirements and, unlike their parents, they are also growing. Gradually their diet will change to become more in line with that of an adult diet, lower in fat, particularly saturated fat, and higher in fibre. It is helpful to think of food groups rather than individual foods. The foods at the bottom of the pyramid are the ones we should be eating more of and we should aim to eat less food from the food groups near the top.

Fats, oils and sweets use in moderation

Milk, yoghurt and cheese 2-3 servings

Meat, poultry, fish, dry beans, eggs and nuts 2-3 servings

Vegetables and fruits 5 servings

Bread, cereal, rice and pasta 6-11 servings

A balanced diet should contain approximately 20% protein, 35% fat, 45% carbohydrate

CARBOHYDRATES

These are the body's main source of energy and also provide vitamins, minerals and fibre. Bread, pasta, potatoes and rice can be used as the basis for many quick, healthy meals. Many people believe starchy foods like bread and potatoes are high in calories, but this is not true. Plain boiled new potatoes are not fattening but adding lots of butter to a baked potato can double its calorie content. A slice of bread contains about 65 calories but buttering it increases this to 142 calories and spreading jam on top adds another 39 calories. Of course, this is less important for children who need more fat in their diet under the age of five, unless overweight. Wholegrain cereals and breads boost your intake of iron, vitamins and fibre.

There are two types of carbohydrates: sugars and starches. In both types there are two forms again.

Sugars: natural fruits and vegetables
refined sugars and honey, soft drinks, cakes, biscuits, jam, confectionery.

Starches: *Complex carbohydrates:* wholegrain breakfast cereal, wholemeal bread and flour, brown rice, potatoes, peas, bananas and many other fruits and vegetables.
Refined carbohydrates: processed breakfast cereals, white flour, bread and pasta, white rice, biscuits and cakes.

It is the complex carbohydrates and natural sugars that should form at least 50% of the calories in your diet.

Refined carbohydrates like white bread and processed sweet breakfast cereals have lost many of their valuable nutrients during processing. Eat more complex carbohydrates, these are energy-rich foods, they keep your blood sugar level constant because they release their sugar content into the bloodstream slowly. They also retain their vitamins and minerals and contain fibre, which encourages the elimination of toxins in the body.

See Vitamins on page 23 for information on fruits and vegetables.

PROTEIN

It is reassuring to know that protein deficiency is almost unheard of in this country and most of us eat more protein than we need. Protein is essential for growth and repair of body tissue and an inadequate supply of protein can lower resistance to disease and infection. The major protein foods are meat, chicken, fish, eggs, dairy products, beans and lentils. It is good to serve one of these foods for lunch and supper. It's also quite likely that you might serve protein foods like cheese or eggs at breakfast too. Protein should make up to 15 – 20% of your daily diet.

As a rough guide, eat meat or chicken 3-4 times a week, and it is recommended that two portions of fish are eaten each week, one of which should be an oily variety like mackerel, tuna, salmon or sardines. These and other oily fish are high in omega-3 fatty acids, which help lower blood pressure, and there is evidence that these fatty acids may help to protect against heart disease and strokes. Sardines are also a good source of bone-strengthening calcium and vitamin B12.

FOODS CONTAINING FAT, FOODS CONTAINING SUGAR

Cakes, biscuits, sweets, crisps and soft drinks fall into this group. As they often contain large quantities of fat, sugar and salt, they should only be eaten occasionally and in small amounts. For adults and children over five, fat should provide no more than 35% of their total calorie intake. The way to achieve this is to cut down on junk food, cakes and biscuits. However, it's not realistic to ban these types of food altogether and they are perfectly fine as occasional foods or part of a meal.

Fats in moderation are an essential part of our diet. Fat makes food more palatable and plays an important role in providing energy, particularly in the diets of young children. It also facilitates the absorption of the fat-soluble vitamins A, D, E and K. Vegetable oils and fish provide the essential fatty acids that the body cannot manufacture from other constituents in the diet.

There are two types of fat: saturated and unsaturated. Saturated fat is derived mainly from animal sources, eg meat, butter, cheese, eggs and margarine, and unsaturated fat come from vegetable sources, eg olive oil, sunflower oil, soft polyunsaturated margarine and oily fish like mackerel. We all need a certain amount of fat in our diet but it is the type of fat that is important. Saturated fats can increase blood cholesterol levels and high intakes are linked to heart disease. It is a good idea to choose lean meats and vegetable oils for frying rather than butter. Cheese contains saturated fat; it is also a good source of calcium, protein and vitamins.

FIVE PORTIONS A DAY

Health experts recommend that we should try to include five portions of fruit and vegetables in our diet every day. This helps to protect against cancers and heart disease and provides the right balance of vitamins, minerals and fibre. As well as providing vitamins and minerals, fruit and vegetables also contain many other biologically active substances called phytochemicals. There is growing scientific evidence for the anti-cancer effects of the 500 phytochemicals identified so far and there may be thousands more.

Different fruits and vegetables contain different vitamins and minerals so try to include as much variety as you can. Fruits, vegetables and juice high in vitamin C help iron to be absorbed from other foods, so ensure you

and your family eat some at each meal. Also fruit and vegetables are low in fat and calories and provide a natural source of fibre, which helps to keep the digestive system in order. Vitamin supplements contain only a small proportion of the benefits available in fruits and vegetables themselves.

Potatoes, sweet potatoes and yams are not included as they are starchy carbohydrates and are categorized as complex carbohydrates. However, other root vegetables are included. Below is a rough guide to show portion size, but this will vary according to age, size, appetite and your own needs.

One serving of fruit :

1 large fruit, apple, banana or orange
2 small fruits, kiwi, apricot
about 20 raspberries
about 7 strawberries
75 g (3 oz) chopped, cooked or canned fruit
45 g (1½ oz) dried fruit
185 ml (6 fl oz) fruit juice

One serving of vegetables :

50 g (2 oz) raw leafy vegetables
75 g (3 oz) cooked or chopped raw vegetables
185 ml (6 fl oz) vegetable juice
a large bowl of salad, eg lettuce, tomato, cucumber, salad cress

Here's an example of how to include five a day:

Fresh fruit juice at breakfast
1 apple, orange or banana with breakfast
Stir-fried vegetables with lunch
Vegetable soup with dinner
Pile extra vegetables on to pizzas

HOW TO CHOOSE A HEALTHY DIET

Foods	Choose more often	Choose less often
Meat, poultry, fish, shellfish, nuts and seeds	Lean cuts of meat trimmed of fat, poultry without skin, fish and shellfish, lean luncheon meat, tinned tuna, sardines, seeds, nuts.	Fatty cuts of meat, bacon and sausage, organ meats, fried chicken, high-fat luncheon meat
Eggs and dairy products	Live and natural yoghurt, low-fat yoghurt and semi-skimmed milk for adults, lower fat cheese (eg cottage cheese, Edam, low-fat Cheddar), boiled or poached eggs.	Cream, full-fat cheese (for adults), fried eggs, processed cheese.
Fats and oils	Soft polyunsaturated fats like margarine, sunflower, grapeseed, safflower, sesame, soya, rapeseed, corn, olive oils.	Saturated fats like butter, lard, suet, hard margarine.
Breads, cereals, pasta, rice, lentils, beans, biscuits, cakes	Wholegrain bread, wholegrain breakfast cereal, pasta and rice, dried beans and lentils, baked goods made with unsaturated oil or margarine, plain biscuits.	White bread, refined sugar-coated cereals, sugary biscuits, cakes, croissants.
Vegetables	Fresh or frozen, raw vegetables, salads, stir-fried vegetables, dark leafy greens and deep yellow or orange vegetables are particularly good.	Fried vegetables (eg chips, crisps), vegetables cooked with a lot of butter (eg mashed potato).
Fruits	Fresh, frozen, canned or dried fruit, pure fruit juice, eat a wide variety of fruits – citrus and berry fruits are particularly good.	Canned fruit in syrup, fruit juice with added sugar, fruit squash, creamy fruit deserts.
Sweet foods	Good quality ice cream, frozen yoghurt, fresh fruit lollies, cereal and dried fruit bars.	Sweets, creamy desserts, chocolates, jelly, sugary ice lollies, soft drinks.

CALCIUM

Calcium is important for the health and formation of bones and teeth and is therefore particularly important for growing children. Calcium is also important for smooth functioning of the muscles, including the heart. Many teenagers are significantly deficient in calcium, which is vital to help build healthy bones during the teenage period of rapid growth. Between 12 and 16 years for girls and 13 and 18 years for boys is a crucial period of bone and muscle growth.

Wheat bran, high-fibre cereals and the tannin in tea and coffee can hinder the absorption of calcium. So if you drink tea or coffee, leave a sufficient gap before or after your meal.

Dairy foods provide the best source of calcium. Two-thirds of a pint of milk a day or equivalent as yoghurt, cheese or milk puddings provides adequate calcium between the ages of one and five. Babies and young children should always be given full-fat milk and dairy products as they contain essential nutrients for early growth.

Other moderately good sources: *dark green leafy vegetables, tofu, sardines, sesame seeds and nuts.*

IRON

Iron deficiency is the commonest nutritional problem in the developed world. Iron's main function is to carry oxygen from the lungs to all the cells in the body. Iron also helps to increase our resistance to infection and aids the healing process. Lack of adequate iron can lead to anaemia, which will result in tiredness and lack of energy. Women, particularly teenage women, need to ensure there is enough iron in their diet as it is lost in the blood during menstruation. Girls who are dieting and those who switch to a vegetarian diet are particularly at risk.

There are two types of iron – one is found in foods of animal origin like red meat or oily fish and is easily absorbed by the body, and the other is found in foods of plant origin like green vegetables or wholegrain cereals

and this is more difficult for the body to absorb. However, including a good source of vitamin C at the same meal, like a glass of fresh orange juice or sliced kiwi fruit and vegetables like sweet pepper or cauliflower, will help to increase the absorption of iron in non-meat sources. Also, if meat or fish is eaten at the same meal as the plant type of iron, the iron is better absorbed.

By mixing lean meat with dark green leafy vegetables you can improve the absorption of iron from the vegetables by about three times. Since the richest and best-absorbed sources of iron are meats and meat products, vegetarians should be careful to ensure they include enough iron-rich foods and vitamin C in their daily diet. Tea, coffee and bran reduce iron absorption.

Good sources: *red meat, particularly liver, oily fish (like salmon, sardines or mackerel), chicken or turkey (dark meat), pulses (like lentils, baked beans), fortified breakfast cereals, bread, green leafy vegetables, dried fruit (especially apricots).*

SMUGGLING EXTRA MILK

There are plenty of ways to add milk into other foods:

■ make fruit milkshakes

■ mash potatoes with plenty of milk

■ make dishes with cheese sauce, eg cauliflower or cheese macaroni cheese

■ sprinkle grated cheese on pasta

■ offer yoghurt or fromage frais

■ whip a half-set jelly with a tin of evaporated milk

■ serve custard or good quality ice cream with puddings.

Vitamins

There are two types of vitamins: water-soluble – B complex and C; or fat-soluble – A, D, E and K. Water-soluble vitamins except for vitamin B12 cannot be stored in the body, so foods containing these should be eaten daily. They are destroyed by heat and dissolve in water, so foods containing these vitamins should not be overcooked. Fat-soluble vitamins are stored in the body, so excessive intake can be damaging.

Vitamin A:
(includes beta-carotene and retinol): important for growth, fighting infection, healthy skin and hair, strong bones, tooth enamel and night vision.
Good sources of beta-carotene: *carrots, tomatoes, red pepper, apricots, mangoes, cantaloupe melon, sweet potato and dark green leafy vegetables.*
Good sources of retinol: *liver, cheese, eggs.*

B complex vitamins:
important for growth, development of a healthy nervous system, food digestion. No foods except liver and yeast extract contain all of the vitamins in the B group.
Good sources: *meat, eggs, sardines, tofu, dark green leafy vegetables, nuts, yeast extract, dairy produce, wholegrain cereals, bananas.*

Vitamin C:
needed for growth and repair of body tissues, healthy skin and healing of wounds. It is also important because it helps the body to absorb iron.
Good sources: *citrus fruit, strawberries, blackcurrants, blackberries, kiwi fruit, sweet pepper, dark green leafy vegetables, potatoes.*

All in a day's food
Any of the following provides a day's vitamin C intake for the average adult.

1 medium-sized orange
1 medium-sized mango
1 kiwi fruit
1 grapefruit
65 g (2½ oz) raw cauliflower
¼ red pepper, raw
1 medium glass freshly squeezed orange juice

Vitamin D:
this is nicknamed the sunshine vitamin because it can be manufactured by the body when the skin is exposed to sunlight. It is needed to absorb calcium and posphorus for healthy bones and teeth.
Good sources: *salmon, tuna, sardines, milk and dairy products, eggs, margarine.*

Vitamin E:
necessary for the maintenance of the body's cell structure and helps the body to create and maintain red blood cells.
Good sources: *vegetable oils, wheatgerm, nuts.*

VITAMIN C AND SMOKING
An average adult needs about 40 mg vitamin C per day. Smokers need up to three times as much because the chemicals from cigarettes destroy the vitamin.

HOME FREEZING OF COOKED FOODS

When you are preparing a recipe it takes only a little more effort to make enough for several meals. You can then serve part of the food freshly cooked and freeze the extra food in meal-size portions. Recipes in this book suitable for freezing are marked with an ❄.

■ Freeze food promptly as soon as it has cooled to room temperature.

■ Cool foods as quickly as possible before packaging – you can speed up the process by placing the container of food in a large pan of ice water.

■ Freeze and store foods at 0°F (-18°C) or less. It's a good idea to purchase a freezer thermometer that can withstand a wide range of temperatures and check the temperature of your freezer regularly.

■ Always re-heat food until piping hot and then allow to cool down before eating in order to kill off any bacteria.

■ Slightly undercook prepared foods. They will finish cooking when reheated.

■ Never re-freeze meals that have been frozen and never re-heat more than once.

■ Bread wrappers are not sufficiently moisture-vapour resistant to be used for freezing. Use proper freezer bags instead.

■ Label and date all packages.

SALT

A high intake of salt is linked to high blood pressure and heart disease in adults so try to limit the amount of salt you add to food so that children don't develop a taste for it. Use herbs and spices to add flavour and try not to add salt at the table. Processed foods like bottled sauces and processed cheeses tend to be high in salt. Also limit snacks like crisps and salted peanuts.

HOW TO READ FOOD LABELS

When buying processed foods always look carefully at the labels for the list of contents.

■ Try to choose foods that are low in sugar, salt and saturated fat and which do not contain monosodium glutamate, colouring or artificial flavours.
■ Ingredients are listed in order of decreasing weight, so if sugar or saturated fat appear near the top of the list, you may want to think again before buying that product.
■ Sugars can be listed in a variety of guises, among them dextrose, glucose, fructose and glucose syrup.
■ Sweetening food with honey, concentrated fruit juice or brown sugar is no better for your teeth than any other kind of sugar.
■ Often labels break carbohydrates into starch and sugars and it is useful to know that 4 grams of sugar makes 1 teaspoon.
■ Below is a chart to show acceptable content of fat, sugar, fibre and sodium per serving.
■ For a complete main meal or in 100 g (4 oz) of a snack food use the following rules of thumb.

Per serving	A lot	A little
Fat	20 g or more	2 g or less
Saturates	5 g or more	1 g or less
Sugars	10 g or more	2 g or less
Fibre	3 g or more	0.5 g or less
Sodium	0.5 g or more	0.1 g or less

(approved by MAFF and the British Heart Foundation)

A Vegetarian Diet

More and more people are choosing to become vegetarian and a vegetarian diet can be very healthy. However, it is important not to give up meat without replacing it with other sources of the nutrients that meat contains, particularly iron, protein and B vitamins.

Animal proteins, including dairy products, contain all the amino acids that the body needs. However, soya is the only plant-based food that contains all the amino acids. In order to get a high-quality protein at each meal, you should try to include some dairy food or combine different non-animal proteins like grains and pulses, which do not contain all the essential amino acids. There are many vegetarian recipes included in this book.

A healthy vegetarian diet should contain staple foods like wholemeal bread, pasta, potatoes and rice, lots of fresh fruits and vegetables, nuts, seeds and pulses and low-fat non-animal sources of protein, eg tofu and low-fat dairy produce. Take care not to eat too much high fat dairy produce and eggs.

Some teenage girls who start dieting and also choose to become vegetarian, may cut out meat from their diet without replacing it with a suitable plant source of iron. This could cause problems as they are particularly prone to iron deficiency due to the loss of blood as they start their periods (see iron on page 22 for increasing the absorption of iron).

Vitamin B12 is vital for making DNA and is needed for the growth and division of cells. It is only found in foods of animal origin such as meat, poultry, fish, eggs and dairy products. Some breakfast cereals are also fortified with vitamin B12. Vegetarians can obtain sufficient vitamin B12 from eggs and dairy produce but vegans should take supplements or eat foods fortified with the vitamin.

NUTS

Small children can be allergic to a number of foods particularly peanuts, sesame seeds, milk, eggs, wheat, soya, fish and shellfish. Peanuts can trigger one of the worst allergic reactions – anaphylactic shock. The throat swells and breathing becomes difficult. In families with a history of any kind of food allergy, it is best to avoid all products containing peanuts until the child is 3 years old. If there is no allergic history, peanut butter can be used from six months. Because of the danger of inhalation, whole nuts should not be given to young children under 5 years of age.

Caramelised Onion and Gruyère Tart: see page 142 for recipe.

Breakfast
Suggestions

Breakfast

The first meal of the day is also the most important. It will probably have been at least 12 hours since your last evening meal and blood sugar levels will be low. If you attempt to skip breakfast then you may suffer various symptoms such as shakiness, headaches and lack of concentration. You will probably then feel hungry later in the morning and crave something sweet, which is your body telling you that it needs glucose fast. It is much better, particularly for children who have high energy and nutrient requirements and who have a long morning at school ahead of them, to start the day with a balanced nutritious breakfast. Here's how to make sure that your child gets a good balanced nutritious breakfast.

FRUIT AND FRUIT JUICE

Choose a wide variety of seasonal fruits. Make fresh fruit salads or a mixture of berries served with some yoghurt and honey or prepare a colourful fruit plate. Berry and citrus fruits are particularly good in your child's diet. Breakfast should supply a good mix of both starch and sugars. Sugar is best provided in the form of fruit or fruit juice, which is quickly broken down into glucose to raise energy levels as well as providing vitamin C, which helps to boost immunity.

BREAD, GRAINS, NUTS AND SEEDS

Starch is ideally provided in bread and/or cereals for longer lasting energy; try to aim for some unrefined starches like whole-grain cereals and bread. If your child is hooked on sugar-coated cereals, try mixing them with some whole-grain cereals like Bran Flakes, Shreddies or Cornflakes. Nuts (for older children) and seeds also contain important nutrients and will help your child to absorb the calcium in his food, so adding extras like sunflower seeds, sesame seeds and chopped nuts to cereals will boost their nutritional content. All bread is nutritious – in Britain, by law white bread flour is fortified with vitamin B, nicotinic acid, iron and calcium and some also have added folate, which is especially important in pregnancy. However, the higher vitamin, mineral and fibre content of wholemeal bread makes it the healthiest choice.

PROTEIN

Try to pick at least one calcium-rich protein food such as milk, yoghurt or cheese every day. Choose whole-milk rather than low-fat varieties for children under 5 unless they are overweight. Eggs are an excellent source of protein and iron for your child and are very versatile.

Eggs should be served to young children with the white and yolk cooked until solid.

BREAKFAST CEREALS

A bowl of cereal is a healthy start to the day for your child but you will need to choose carefully. Many of the cereals designed to appeal to children are highly refined and packed full of sugar (some contain almost 50% sugar). Ignore claims about added vitamins and minerals – vitamins are added to replace losses during processing. It is much better to choose whole-wheat cereals that are not coated in sugar like Weetabix, Ready Brek and porridge. Even if your child adds some sugar it will still be a lot less than the 4 to 5 teaspoons you might find in some cereals. Eating cereal also ensures your children get milk, which provides both protein and calcium.

> **TIP**
> Very fresh eggs will contain fewer bacteria than older eggs so try to find eggs that display the date on which they were laid. Elderly people, pregnant women and very young children should not eat lightly cooked or raw eggs.

Quick Breakfasts

FRUIT SALAD WITH HONEY YOGHURT DRESSING

Make a fruit salad using seasonal fruits and top with a mixture of Greek yoghurt and honey. Alternatively, make a fruit plate and serve with a bowl of yoghurt and honey for dipping.

STEWED FRUIT

Stewed fruit, like cooking apple cooked with a little brown sugar and cinnamon or rhubarb with some fresh orange juice and brown sugar, makes a nice change for breakfast. Alternatively, make a baked apple with honey, raisins and a knob of butter and serve it cold for breakfast.

BREAKFAST CEREAL PLUS

Adding fresh fruits or dried fruits like chopped dried apricots to breakfast cereals will give sweetness without the need for sugar.

FUNNY SHAPE FRENCH TOAST

Lightly beat together 1 egg and 30 ml (2 tbsp) of milk. Cut the bread into shapes using novelty cookie cutters and fry in butter until golden.

BOILED EGGS WITH SOLDIERS

Place the eggs in a saucepan, cover with cold water and place on a high heat. Bring to the boil and then reduce the heat to a simmer and cook for between 4 and 5 minutes. Serve surrounded by fingers of toast, spread with a little butter and Marmite. They are delicious dipped into the egg.

DRIED FRUIT COMPOTES

Many supermarkets stock a selection of ready-to-eat dried fruits. Put the fruit into a saucepan, cover with water, bring to the boil and simmer until soft (about 10 minutes). You can add a cinnamon stick to flavour the fruit if you like. It's also nice to mix in some fresh fruits like apples, pears or oranges. Add these towards the end of the cooking time as they will cook much faster. Fruit compotes can be made ahead and served cold.

TOAST WITH PEANUT BUTTER, HONEY AND BANANAS

Spread slices of toasted granary bread with peanut butter and a little honey and top with a thinly sliced banana.

FRUITY MILKSHAKES

Blend together fresh fruit and milk to make delicious milkshakes. Try combinations like fresh strawberries, banana and milk, peaches, nectarines or fresh dates and banana. For a richer milkshake, add a refreshing scoop of ice cream.

SCRAMBLED EGGS PLUS

Make scrambled eggs extra special by adding ingredients like chopped tomatoes, grated cheese or ham. These should be added one minute before the eggs are done.

BREAKFAST SUNDAE

Into a sundae glass spoon layers of yoghurt, fresh fruit (such as mixed berries) and crunchy breakfast cereal until the glass is full.

Strawberry and Banana Yoghurt Shake

Makes 1 tall glass

1 small banana, peeled and sliced
4 strawberries

30 ml (2 tbsp) orange juice
1 x 150 g (5 oz) pot vanilla yoghurt

Put the banana, strawberries and orange juice into a blender or food processor and purée. Add the yoghurt and purée until smooth.

Swirly Porridge

A warm bowl of porridge makes a satisfying and nourishing breakfast and will help to keep energy levels up until lunchtime. The soluble fibre in oats is believed to help lower blood cholesterol levels. You can try adding a little honey, golden syrup, raisins, dried apricots, strawberries, raspberries or even peaches to vary the flavour of the porridge. A 25 g (1 oz) serving of porridge made with skimmed milk provides a good low-fat breakfast.

Makes 2 bowls porridge

50 g (2 oz) porridge oats
460 ml (16 fl oz) milk (or water)

30 ml (2 tbsp) strawberry jam
blueberries or raspberries

Mix the oats with the milk or water in a saucepan. Bring to the boil and then simmer, stirring occasionally, for 5 minutes. Stir the strawberry jam in a bowl until it turns runny and then drizzle it in a spiral pattern on to the cereal. Add some blueberries to decorate the spiral pattern.

Muesli with Yoghurt, Honey and Fruit

Makes 1 portion

3 tablespoons muesli
1 x 150 g (5 oz) pot natural yoghurt
10 ml (2 tsp) honey

fresh fruit, such as raspberries,
peaches, blueberries

Simply mix together the muesli, yoghurt and honey and top with the fresh fruit. Larger fruits such as strawberries or peaches are best cut into small pieces.

Best-ever Banana Bread

This banana bread is wonderfully moist and is great for breakfast or lunchboxes. This keeps well but you can also wrap slices in plastic wrap and freeze in plastic freezer bags. Many children aren't keen on nuts, so you can omit them from this recipe. Nut allergies are also a very real problem (see page 25).

Makes 8 slices

100 g (4 oz) butter
100 g (4 oz) brown sugar
1 egg
450 g (1 lb) bananas, mashed
45 ml (3 tbsp) natural yoghurt
5 ml (1 tsp) vanilla essence

225 g (8 oz) plain flour
1 teaspoon bicarbonate of soda
1 teaspoon ground cinnamon
¼ teaspoon salt
100 g (4 oz) raisins
40 g (1½ oz) chopped pecans or walnuts (optional)

Pre-heat the oven to 180°C/350°F/Gas 4 and grease and line a 22 x 11 x 7 cm (8½ x 4¼ x 2¾ in) loaf tin. Beat the butter and sugar together until creamy then add the egg and continue to beat until smooth. Add the mashed bananas, yoghurt and vanilla essence.

Sift together the flour, bicarbonate of soda, cinnamon and salt and beat this gradually into the banana mixture. Finally, stir in the raisins and chopped nuts (if using). Bake for about 1 hour or until a cocktail stick inserted in the centre comes out clean.

TIP

If time is short in the morning, get some of the breakfast organised the night before. Have cereal ready in bowls, perhaps prepare a muesli and keep it in the fridge overnight and simply stir in some fresh fruit in the morning or bake some banana bread the day before and have it ready on the table. If your child is really rushed in the morning, let him take some portable food with him on the way to school like a banana, home-baked muffins or some dried apricots.

Cheesy Bread Shapes

These are good fun for children to make as they love to knead the dough and mould it into animal shapes. On a cool morning, you might like to consider warming them in the oven before eating.

Makes 6 bread shapes

225 g (8 oz) strong plain flour plus flour to dust
a pinch of salt
½ tablespoon fast action dried yeast
½ teaspoon caster sugar
1 teaspoon dried mustard powder
1 teaspoon vegetable oil
400 ml (⅔ pint) warm water
25 g (1 oz) Red Leicestershire cheese, grated
25 g (1 oz) mature Cheddar cheese, grated
1 spring onion, finely chopped

To decorate

1 egg, beaten
currants
grated cheese
sesame seeds
poppy seeds

Sift the flour, mustard and salt into a bowl. Place the yeast in a mixing bowl, pour over the warm water, stir in the sugar and mix with a fork. Allow to stand until the yeast has dissolved and starts to foam (about 10 minutes). Stir in the oil and gradually mix in the flour mixture. If the dough is sticky, add a little extra flour. Transfer to a floured work surface and knead gently for about 5 minutes to make a smooth, pliable dough. Gradually knead the grated cheese and spring onion into the dough to give it a streaky effect.

Shape the dough into rolls or animal shapes and put them on to a greased baking tray. Cover loosely with a tea-towel and then put them in a warm place to rise for about 1 hour or until doubled in size.

Pre-heated the oven to 200°C/400°F/Gas 6. Brush the shapes with beaten egg and add currants for eyes. Sprinkle the tops with grated cheese, sesame seeds or poppy seeds. Bake in an oven for 15 to 20 minutes or until golden. They are done if they sound hollow when tapped underneath. Transfer to a wire rack to cool.

Welsh Rarebit

This is the perfect mixture for a really tasty Welsh Rarebit. I like the flavour when it is made with beer and I sometimes add 30 ml (2 tbsp) beer. However, for young children you may prefer to use milk instead. The addition of the egg gives this a firm but lovely light texture. This makes a good breakfast or snack.

Makes 4 portions

4 slices thick wholemeal toast
25 g (1 oz) butter
175 g (6 oz) Cheddar cheese, grated
15 ml (1 tbsp) beer or milk

½ teaspoon dried mustard powder
salt and freshly ground black pepper
1 egg yolk
paprika for sprinkling

Melt the butter in a saucepan. Add the cheese, beer or milk, the mustard and a little seasoning. Remove from the heat and beat in the egg yolk. Toast the bread and lay on a baking tray or on a grill pan on a sheet of kitchen foil. Spoon the mixture on to each slice of toast and sprinkle with a little paprika. Place under a pre-heated grill to brown quickly and then serve at once.

Cheese, Chive and Tomato Omelette

This is a delicious folded omelette, flavoured with chives and filled with fresh tomatoes and melted cheese. If you don't have any chives, then make a herb omelette using ¼ teaspoon mixed dried herbs. Eggs are a good source of protein and are rich in vitamins and minerals.

Makes 1 portion

2 eggs
½ tablespoon snipped chives
salt and freshly ground black pepper

15 g (½ oz) butter
2 tomatoes, skinned and roughly chopped
25 g (1 oz) Cheddar or Gruyère cheese, grated

Beat the eggs with the chives and season with a little salt and freshly ground black pepper. Melt the butter in a 20 cm (8 in) frying pan, add the beaten egg and chives and swirl the mixture around to coat the pan evenly.

When the edges of the egg begin to set, lift the egg with a spatula, tilt the pan towards the edge you have lifted and let the uncooked egg flow underneath the cooked portion.

Place the pan back on the burner. Spoon the tomatoes and grated cheese on to one side of the omelette. Fold over and cook for about 1 minute over a gentle heat until the omelette is set and the cheese is melted.

Perfect Pancakes

Pancakes for breakfast are a real treat and you can make delicious, really thin pancakes with this foolproof batter.
Sprinkle them with lemon juice and dust with icing sugar or serve with maple or golden syrup and perhaps some fresh
fruit. These pancakes can be made in advance, refrigerated and then re-heated just before serving. Pancakes also freeze
very well. Interleave with non-stick baking paper, then wrap in foil and freeze for up to a month. Thaw at room
temperature for several hours.

Makes 12 pancakes

100 g (4 oz) plain flour
a generous pinch of salt
2 eggs
300 ml (½ pint) milk
50 g (2 oz) melted butter

> **MENU PLANNING**
> *Breakfast need not just mean a bowl of cereal and*
> *toast.*
> *See the Planners on pages 10-16.*

S ift the flour with a big pinch of salt into a mixing bowl, make a well in the centre and add the eggs. Use a balloon
whisk to incorporate the eggs into the flour and gradually whisk in the milk. Stir the mixture until smooth but do not
over mix.

Use a heavy bottomed 15-18 cm (6-7 in) frying pan and brush with the melted butter (either use a pastry brush or dip
some crumpled kitchen towel into the butter to coat the base of the pan) and when hot, pour in about 30 ml (2 tbsp) of
the batter. Quickly tilt the pan from side to side until you get a thin layer of batter covering the base of the frying pan.
Cook the pancake for about 1 minute, then flip it over (you can use a spatula for this) and cook until the underside is lightly flecked with gold. Continue with the rest of the batter, brushing the pan with melted butter when necessary.

French Toast

Makes 2 portions

2 thick slices of day-old white bread
1 large egg

30 ml (2 tbsp) milk
25 g (1 oz) butter

B eat together the egg and milk and pour into a shallow dish. Cut the bread into triangles or cut out shapes using cookie cutters. Dip the bread into the mixture and fry in the butter until golden. Serve with fruit or a fruit compote (see
Dried Fruit Compotes on page 29) and dust with a little icing or caster sugar.

Savoury Breakfast Muffins

Cheese and tomato on toast makes a nutritious breakfast and using split toasted muffins makes a nice variation. You can vary the toppings depending on what you have on hand in the kitchen. (*See photograph opposite*)

Makes 1 or 2 portions

1 muffin
a little butter or margarine
1 tomato, sliced thinly
salt and freshly ground black pepper
50 g (2 oz) Cheddar cheese, grated

Decoration (optional)
thinly sliced ham
2 cherry tomatoes
2 slices cucumber
1 black olive
slice of red pepper

Split and toast the muffin. Spread with a little butter or margarine. Arrange some thinly sliced tomato on top, lightly season and then cover with the grated cheese. Place under a pre-heated grill until lightly golden. If you wish, you can then have some fun decorating them to look like faces.

Apple and Carrot Breakfast Muffins

Here is a healthy and deliciously moist muffin that's bound to become a family favourite. These muffins are very easy to make and will keep well for up to 5 days. They are also great for lunchboxes or as a snack for any time of the day.

Makes 12 muffins

150 g (5 oz) plain wholemeal flour
50 g (2 oz) granulated sugar
25 g (1 oz) dried skimmed milk powder
1½ teaspoons baking powder
½ teaspoon cinnamon
¼ teaspoon salt
¼ teaspoon ginger
125 ml (4 fl oz) vegetable oil

60 ml (2 fl oz) honey
60 ml (2 fl oz) maple syrup
2 eggs, lightly beaten
2.5 ml (½ tsp) vanilla essence
1 large apple, peeled and grated
75 g (3 oz) carrots, peeled and grated
65 g (2½ oz) raisins

Pre-heat the oven to 180°C/350°F/Gas 4. Combine the flour, sugar, skimmed milk powder, baking powder, cinnamon, salt and ginger in a mixing bowl. In a separate bowl combine the oil, honey, maple syrup, eggs and vanilla essence. Beat lightly with a wire whisk until blended. Add the grated apple, carrots and raisins to the liquid mixture and stir well. Fold in the dry ingredients until just combined but don't over mix or the muffins will become heavy.

Line a muffin tray with paper cups and fill the muffin cups until two-thirds full. Bake for 20 to 25 minutes.

Fruity Homemade Muesli

So many of the breakfast cereals designed specifically for children are very high in sugar and low in nutrients. However, it's very easy to make your own delicious muesli using porridge oats, fresh and dried fruits and fresh fruit juices. There are now many delicious fresh fruit juices available in supermarkets, which can be used to soak and flavour the grains. This makes a nutritious alternative and you can add fresh fruit depending on the season. *(See photograph opposite)*

Makes 4 portions

150 g (5 oz) porridge oats
50 g (2 oz) toasted wheat germ
25 g (1 oz) each dried peaches and apricots, finely chopped
25 g (1 oz) raisins

375 ml (12 fl oz) apple and mango juice or apple juice
1 apple, peeled and grated
fresh fruit, such as strawberries, raspberries, peaches

S oak the muesli base or oats, toasted wheat germ and dried fruit in the juice for at least 20 minutes or overnight. Stir in the grated apple and the fruit of your choice.

Lemon and Raisin Drop Scones

These mini drop scones are quick and easy to prepare and children will enjoy helping to make them. They are also excellent for tea-time. To serve from frozen, defrost, wrap in aluminium foil and warm through in a medium oven.

Makes about 10 scones

100 g (4 oz) self-raising flour
1 teaspoon baking powder
3 tablespoons caster sugar
1 egg
150 ml (¼ pint) milk
grated rind of 1 small lemon

75 g (3 oz) raisins
oil for greasing

> **MENU PLANNING**
> *The perfect accompaniment for cereal and fruit.*
> *See Spring Planner, page 10*

S ift the flour, baking powder and sugar into a mixing bowl. Make a well in the centre and crack the egg into it. Using a whisk, beat the egg, gradually drawing in the flour, and slowly add the milk, whisking all the time to form a smooth batter. Stir in the lemon zest and raisins.

Lightly grease a large heavy frying pan and when hot, drop 45-60 ml (3-4 tbsp) of the batter into the pan, keeping the drop scones well apart. Cook for 2 to 3 minutes, then flip them over and cook for about 1 minute or until golden underneath. Keep the pancakes warm by wrapping in kitchen paper while you use up the rest of the batter. Serve warm with maple syrup.

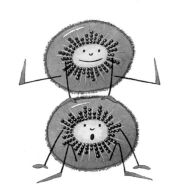

Soups, Snacks
and Lunchboxes

Soups, Snacks and Lunchboxes

PACKED LUNCHES

The nutritional quality of school meals varies tremendously and if you are unhappy with your child's school meals and are unable to effect any real changes to be sure that your child is getting a good balanced meal, a packed lunch may well be the sensible answer. Often fussy eaters will find nothing that they like to eat in the school dining room and may end up with eating very little for their lunch, with the consequence that they have no energy and lack concentration as the day wears on.

It can be quite a challenge to come up with new ideas for your child's lunchbox that will entice her or him to eat and bring a smile to your child's face. Simple touches can make all the difference, like drawing a face on a banana with a felt-tipped pen or wrapping sandwiches in foil and decorating them with stickers.

Warm conditions encourage the growth of bacteria so it's important to keep lunchboxes cool. For the summer months it's worth getting a lunchbox with a built-in ice pack to keep food fresh. Alternatively, you could put a carton of juice in the freezer, transfer it to your child's lunchbox in the morning and by lunchtime it will have defrosted but will have helped to keep your child's food fresh.

SANDWICHES

There is an endless variety of types of sandwiches that you can make for your child's lunchbox. For example, there are now many different types of bread available in supermarkets, such as mini round pitta bread, ciabatta, bridge rolls, bagels, French bread, naan bread, raisin bread, onion or sun-dried tomato bread. To stop the bread from going soggy you can put lettuce leaves between the bread and the filling. Bread doesn't always need to be buttered, especially if you use ingredients like cream cheese or peanut butter instead. Also, there is no need to always make square or triangular sandwiches.

So, below and opposite are some ideas to make an ordinary sandwich into something special to delight your child. Wrap sandwiches in non-PVC plastic wrap or aluminium foil or pack them in small plastic boxes to prevent them from getting squashed.

PINWHEEL SANDWICHES

When making these, choose a contrasting coloured filling to the colour of the bread – something like smoked salmon or avocado and cream cheese. To make a pinwheel sandwich, choose a fairly dense bread and if you can chill it first it will make it easier to handle. First remove the crusts from two slices of bread. Then place the slices on a board, slightly overlapping the shorter edges, and roll them together with a rolling pin to join the slices together and to make the bread more pliable. Spread with your chosen filling and roll up like a swiss roll. Using a sharp knife, slice into wheels. If making these ahead, wrap tightly with plastic wrap and set aside in the fridge and then slice just before serving.

DOUBLE-DECKER SANDWICHES

Use three slices of bread, two white and one brown. Spread one slice of white bread with peanut butter and arrange some sliced bananas on top. Butter both sides of the brown bread and spread one side with strawberry jam. Place jam side up on top of the first slice and top with the remaining slice of white bread. Trim the crusts and cut into three strips. Cut the strips into three again to form nine mini double-decker sandwiches. You can use any two fillings that complement each other, such as cream cheese and cucumber, egg mayonnaise and lettuce, and tomato, ham and cheese.

Lunchbox Suggestions

✓ Crunchy raw vegetables with a tasty dip. Dips with crunchy vegetables such as carrots, celery, cucumber, sweet pepper and cherry tomatoes are very popular with children. A bundle of vegetables can be wrapped up in plastic wrap or you can thread a variety of vegetables on to small wooden skewers. There is a large selection of ready-made dips now available in supermarkets and these could be turned into small plastic cartons like used cottage cheese or fromage frais pots for transportation.

✓ Miniature cheeses from the supermarket pick and mix selection.

✓ Yoghurt and fromage frais.

✓ A slice of pizza.

✓ Raisins and cashew nut mix.

✓ Dried fruit such as apricots. You can make fruit kebabs with different fruits, alternating fresh and dried.

✓ Hard-boiled eggs.

✓ Chicken skewers – there are quite a variety in this book (see Teriyaki or Yakitori Chicken Skewers on pages 81 and 94) and they can be prepared the night before and refrigerated. These skewers are just as good cold as hot.

✓ Many supermarkets have individually wrapped snacks that are ideal to drop straight into your child's lunchbox. Try such items as cheese strings, twin cartons of cream cheese with miniature breadsticks for dipping and miniature boxes of raisins.

✓ Vegetable crisps: you can buy packets of crispy carrot, parsnip, sweet potato and beetroot seasoned with sea salt.

✓ Oatcakes and other plain biscuits.

✓ Cereal bars.

✓ A piece of fruit.

✓ Home-made or bought soup in a flask.

Sandwich fillings

Try all or any of the following:

✓ Peanut butter and strawberry or raspberry jam

✓ Peanut butter, honey and sliced bananas

✓ Strawberry jam and plain Quark cheese

✓ Cream cheese and cucumber

✓ Butter and Marmite, shredded lettuce, grated Cheddar cheese

✓ Peanut butter or chocolate spread and sliced banana

✓ Cheddar cheese with chutney, pickle or sliced pickled or fresh cucumber

✓ Mashed sardines in tomato sauce

✓ Hard-boiled egg mashed with a little soft margarine and mayonnaise and sprinkled with chopped salad cress, alfalfa sprouts or some finely chopped celery

✓ Hummus, grated carrot and sliced cucumber

✓ Cream cheese and chopped dried apricot

✓ Taramasalata

✓ Tuna mayonnaise with chopped celery

✓ Mashed sardines mixed with a little Tomato Ketchup

✓ Roast chicken or beef with salad in pockets of pitta bread

✓ Sliced turkey, salad and Swiss cheese

Lara's Lovely Onion Soup

My daughter Lara loves onion soup and this one has a delicious flavour as I allow the onions to caramelise to bring out their flavour. You can mix ordinary onions with red onions if you like. It's great comfort food on a cold winter's night.

Makes 8 portions

30 ml (2 tbsp) olive oil
50 g (2 oz) butter
550 g (1¼ lb) onions, thinly sliced
1 clove garlic, crushed
½ teaspoon granulated sugar
1.2 litres (2 pints) good beef stock

1 large potato, peeled and cubed
150 ml (¼ pint) dry white wine
salt and freshly ground black pepper
½ French loaf
75 g (3 oz) Gruyère cheese, grated

TIP

For winter, it's a good idea to include something hot in your child's lunchbox, so invest in a small Thermos flask that you could fill with soup. There are many delicious home-made soups to try, or perhaps heat up a small can of baked beans and use that to fill a Thermos flask.

Melt the oil and butter in a large casserole. Add the onions, garlic and sugar, and cook over a medium heat, stirring until the onions have browned. Reduce the heat to the lowest setting, cover the onions with a sheet of non-stick baking paper and leave the onions to cook slowly for 30 minutes.

Meanwhile, put 600 ml (1 pint) of the stock into a saucepan, add the chopped potato and cook for 10 to 12 minutes or until the potato is soft. Blend the potato with some of the stock in a food processor or blender. This will help to thicken the soup.

Remove the non-stick baking paper and pour the thickened stock, the remaining beef stock and the wine over the caramelised onions. Season, then stir with a wooden spoon, scraping the base of the pan to get the full flavour of the caramelised onions. Simmer gently uncovered for 30 minutes.

To make the cheesy French bread slices to float on top of the soup, first cut the loaf diagonally into 12 mm (½ in) slices and toast lightly on both sides. Pour the soup into individual oven-proof bowls and top each one with a slice of bread. Sprinkle the bread liberally with the grated cheese. Place the bowls under a hot grill until the cheese is melted and bubbling. Serve immediately.

Tasty and Healthy Vegetable Soup

A good home-made vegetable soup can be a great way to encourage reluctant vegetable eaters to eat more. This is one of my favourite combinations.

Makes 8 portions

25 g (1 oz) butter
1 medium onion, chopped
400 g (14 oz) carrots, peeled and chopped
225 g (8 oz) potato, peeled and chopped
1.2 litres (2 pints) good chicken or vegetable stock
150 g (5 oz) button mushrooms, chopped
1 celery stalk, chopped

1 clove garlic, crushed
½ teaspoon sugar
1½ teaspoons snipped fresh thyme or ½ teaspoon dried thyme
salt and freshly ground black pepper

Melt the butter in a large casserole or saucepan and sauté the onion until softened and lightly golden. Stir in the carrots and potato and cook, stirring, for 2 minutes. Pour over the stock and add the mushrooms, celery, garlic, sugar and thyme. Bring to the boil, then reduce the heat and cover and simmer for about 50 minutes. Liquidise in a blender and season to taste.

Nourishing Lentil Soup

Lentils are not generally very popular with children but here's a very tasty way to enjoy them. This nutritious soup has proved very popular with my young team of tasters, who never hesitate to give something the thumbs down if it doesn't appeal.

Makes 8 portions

25 g (1 oz) butter
1 medium onion, chopped
1 leek, white part only, finely sliced
1 clove garlic, crushed
225 g (8 oz) carrots, chopped
50 g (2 oz) celery, finely sliced

100 g (4 oz) red lentils
1 medium potato (about 150 g/5 oz), peeled and diced
2 tablespoons fresh chopped parsley
1.75 litres (3 pints) vegetable or chicken stock
salt and freshly ground black pepper

Melt the butter in a large saucepan and sauté the onion, leek, garlic, carrots and celery for about 10 minutes or until softened. Add the lentils, diced potato and parsley and pour the stock into the mixture. Stir and bring to the boil. Season with a little salt and freshly ground black pepper, cover and simmer gently for about 45 minutes. Purée in a blender to a thick, smooth consistency.

Potato, Leek and Watercress Soup

Watercress is an excellent source of the antioxidants betacarotene and vitamin C. I was surprised to find how much my children liked the taste of this soup even though it contains blue cheese, which is quite a sophisticated taste. However, if your children prefer, you can leave out the cheese from their portion.

Makes 5 portions

15 ml (1 tbsp) olive oil
15 g (½ oz) butter
1 large leek, chopped
200 g (7 oz) potato, peeled and diced
900 ml (1½ pints) chicken stock

¼ teaspoon mace
1 teaspoon caster sugar
salt and freshly ground black pepper
2 x 85 g (3½ oz) bags watercress
85-100 g (3½-4 oz) Dolcelatte cheese, cut into cubes

Melt the butter and oil in a pan. Add the leek and potato. Sauté for 4 to 5 minutes until the leek begins to soften. Add the stock, mace, sugar and season with salt and freshly ground black pepper. Cover and cook for 10 minutes. Add the watercress and remove the lid. Simmer for 10 minutes. Add the cheese and blend in a food processor or blender. Check for seasoning.

Mummy's Minestrone

Minestrone is a family favourite in our house. Sometimes, I leave out the baked beans and soup pasta and instead add a can of cartoon character pasta in tomato sauce, which seems to add to its child appeal.

Makes 8 portions

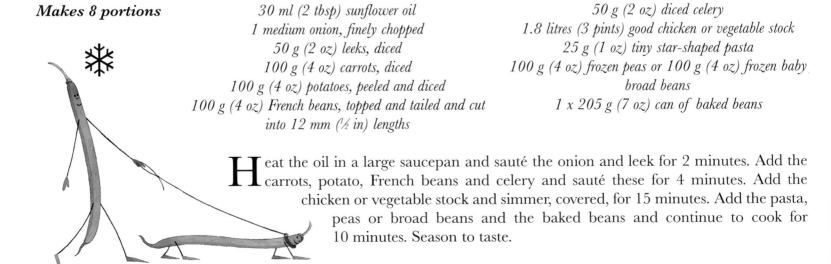

30 ml (2 tbsp) sunflower oil
1 medium onion, finely chopped
50 g (2 oz) leeks, diced
100 g (4 oz) carrots, diced
100 g (4 oz) potatoes, peeled and diced
100 g (4 oz) French beans, topped and tailed and cut into 12 mm (½ in) lengths

50 g (2 oz) diced celery
1.8 litres (3 pints) good chicken or vegetable stock
25 g (1 oz) tiny star-shaped pasta
100 g (4 oz) frozen peas or 100 g (4 oz) frozen baby broad beans
1 x 205 g (7 oz) can of baked beans

Heat the oil in a large saucepan and sauté the onion and leek for 2 minutes. Add the carrots, potato, French beans and celery and sauté these for 4 minutes. Add the chicken or vegetable stock and simmer, covered, for 15 minutes. Add the pasta, peas or broad beans and the baked beans and continue to cook for 10 minutes. Season to taste.

Good Old-fashioned Chicken Soup

This comforting soup is a traditional favourite on the dining table of Jewish households all over the world. It's not only delicious and low in fat but also considered a cure for almost all illnesses and very good for anyone convalescing. Boiler chickens are available from most butchers and if your butcher has any veal bones available, these can also be used to enhance the flavour of the soup. I always like to keep a supply of this soup in my freezer.

It also makes a delicious full-flavoured chicken stock, which can be used as the basis for many other recipes. However, do not defrost the stock and then re-freeze it again in another recipe. It must either be used fresh or not re-frozen.

Makes 8 portions

1 large boiler chicken cut into 8 pieces plus giblets
2.25 litres (4 pints) water
2 large onions, peeled and roughly chopped
3 large carrots, scrubbed and roughly sliced
2 parsnips, scrubbed and roughly chopped
1 leek, sliced
1 stalk celery, chopped
2 sprigs of parsley
2 or 3 chicken stock cubes

MENU PLANNING
Soups are supremely comforting at any time of day in the autumn and winter.
See Autumn and Winter Planners, pages 14 and 16.

Wash the chicken and giblets, trimming away any excess fat. Put into a large pan with the water and bring very slowly to the boil. Simmer for 5 minutes, carefully skimming off any scum that forms on the surface. Add all the remaining ingredients and simmer, covered, for 1½ hours.

Remove the chicken with a slotted spoon, strip off the flesh, reserving it for the soup and return the bones to the pan. Cover and simmer gently for another 1½ hours, then strain. Season to taste. Discard the solids, cool the stock and chill in the fridge overnight and in the morning you can remove the layer of fat that settles on top. You can then add some of the reserved chicken cut into bite-sized pieces and some noodles too if you like.

Cucumber Crocodile

This looks amazing, it's great for parties and it also makes a fabulous prop for your own children's healthy snacks. I like to use a variety of cheeses , but cubes of ham or chicken also work well on in place of the cheese. (*See photograph opposite*)

Serves 4–6

1 cucumber
mixture of cheeses
1 carrot (optional)
fresh pineapple or 1 small can of pineapple chunks

cocktail sticks
2 cherry tomatoes
salad cress (optional)

Cut out a triangle at one end of the cucumber to make the crocodile's mouth. Cut two lengths of cheese and the carrot (if using) and, with a sharp knife, cut along one side of each length to form a serrated edge. These are the crocodile's teeth. Chop the cheeses and pineapple into cubes. Thread cheese and pineapple cubes on to each cocktail stick and spear the sticks into the cucumber. Cut a cocktail stick in half and use the two halves to attach the cherry tomatoes to form the crocodile's eyes. Give the crocodile some teeth and he's ready to be served up! If you like, you can put him on a bed of salad cress to look like grass.

Mediterranean Tomato Soup

This tomato soup has a wonderful flavour and it's a great recipe to encourage children to eat more vegetables. Tomatoes are particularly rich in vitamin C and lycopene (the red pigment), which has been found to help protect against certain forms of cancer, in particular prostate cancer, so it's especially advisable for men to include tomatoes in their diet several times a week. Lycopene is released when tomatoes are cooked and better absorbed with a little oil.

Makes 6 portions

30 ml (2 tbsp) olive oil
25 g (1 oz) butter
2 medium onions, diced
2 medium carrots, peeled and diced
2 celery sticks, diced
1 clove garlic, crushed
1½ tablespoons roughly chopped basil

1½ tablespoons roughly chopped tarragon
1 bay leaf
500 g (1 lb 2 oz) ripe plum tomatoes, skinned,
quartered and de-seeded
1 x 400 g (14 oz) can of chopped tomatoes
15 ml (1 tbsp) tomato purée
600 ml (1 pint) chicken stock

Heat the olive oil and butter in a large saucepan and sauté the onion, carrots and celery for 2 to 3 minutes. Add the garlic, herbs and bay leaf and cook for 7 to 8 minutes. Add the fresh and canned tomatoes and cook over a low heat for about 15 minutes. Stir in the tomato purée and gradually add the stock. Cook over a medium heat for 15 minutes. Remove the bay leaf and blend in a food processor or blender. Season to taste.

Individual Pinwheel Pizzas

These pinwheel pizzas are just the right size for little fingers. They also make tasty morsels for the grown-ups and look much more attractive than offering slices of pizza. These pinwheel pizzas can also be made ahead and frozen. If you don't want to make your own pastry, you can make these with frozen shortcrust pastry.

Makes approximately 12 individual pinwheel pizzas

225 g (8 oz) self-raising flour
¼ teaspoon salt
50 g (2 oz) butter
50 g (2 oz) Cheddar cheese, grated
1 teaspoon mixed herbs
150 ml (¼ pint) milk

Topping

1 medium onion, chopped
100 g (4 oz) button mushrooms, chopped
15 ml (1 tbsp) olive oil
30 ml (2 tbsp) red pesto
30 ml (2 tbsp) tomato purée
75 g (3 oz) Cheddar cheese, grated

Preheat the oven to 180°C/350°F/Gas 4. Sieve together the flour and salt. Using your fingertips, rub in the butter so that it resembles fine breadcrumbs. Stir in the grated cheese and herbs. Stir in the milk until the mixture forms a soft dough. Turn on to a lightly floured surface and knead for 1 minute to make a smooth dough (don't knead for too long or the dough will become greasy).

Roll out the dough on a sheet of non-stick baking paper to a rectangle about 32 x 20 cm (12 x 8 in). Sauté the onion and mushrooms in the olive oil for 3 to 4 minutes. Stir in the pesto and tomato purée. Spread the mushroom and tomato mixture evenly over the rolled out dough and sprinkle over the grated cheese.

Using the baking paper as a guide, roll up the dough from the long side. Remove the baking paper and, using a sharp knife, cut into about 12 slices, each about 2 cm (1¾ in) thick. Place cut side down on a greased baking tray and bake for about 20 minutes or until golden.

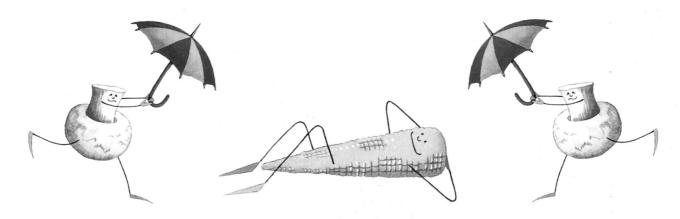

Quick Ciabatta Pizza

Ciabatta is a crusty, open-textured white bread made with olive oil and you can buy half-sized loaves in most supermarkets, which are just the right size for making individual pizzas. Alternatively, cut a full-size loaf in half.

Makes 2 individual pizzas

1 x ½ ciabatta loaf
30 ml (2 tbsp) olive oil
60 ml (4 tbsp) good quality tomato sauce
2 button mushrooms, thinly sliced
2 smallish tomatoes, skinned and sliced
salt and freshly ground black pepper
50 g (2 oz) canned or frozen sweetcorn
40 g (1½ oz) sliced pepperoni (optional)

1 tablespoon shredded fresh basil leaves or ¼ teaspoon mixed herbs
50 g (2 oz) Cheddar cheese, grated

MENU PLANNING
For a light lunch, serve with salad and fruit.
See Spring Planner, page 10.

Pre-heat the oven to 200°C/400°F/Gas 6. Cut the ciabatta loaf in half horizontally and place the two halves on a baking sheet. Drizzle over the olive oil and spread with the tomato sauce.

Scatter over the sliced mushrooms, arrange the tomato slices on top and season with a little salt and pepper. Scatter over the sweetcorn and pepperoni (if using) and sprinkle over the herbs and the grated cheese. Transfer to the oven and cook for about 15 minutes or until bubbling and golden.

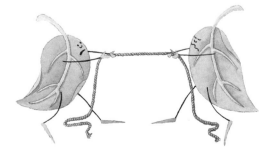

Buzzy Bees

These tasty bees are great fun for parties and they are just the right size for little children. They are packed full of nutritious ingredients and older children will also enjoy making these themselves because they are quick and easy to make and need no cooking. You may want to double the quantity next time around since these bees will keep your children buzzing around for more.

Makes 10 bees

60 ml (4 tbsp) smooth peanut butter
15 ml (1 tbsp) honey
2 tablespoons dried skimmed milk powder
1 tablespoon sesame seeds
1 Weetabix, crushed

Decoration

1 tablespoon cocoa powder
rice paper cut into the shape of wings or flaked almonds
10 currants

Mix together the peanut butter and honey then blend in the remaining ingredients. Form heaped teaspoons of the mixture into oval shapes to look like bees. Dip a toothpick into the cocoa powder and press gently on to the bees' bodies to form stripes.

Press rice paper wings or flaked almonds into the sides of the bee. Cut the currants in half, roll between your finger and thumb to form tiny balls and arrange them on the bees to look like eyes. The bees can be stored in the fridge for several days.

Salad Bar with Soy Sauce Dressing

Salads and a jacket potato can easily become a main meal with the addition of ingredients like grated cheese, chopped egg or chopped chicken. Combined with some delicious freshly baked breads, which can now be bought in the supermarket, fresh fruit and ice cream, it makes an easy and popular meal for the whole family. Sometimes when I have a group of children over for lunch in the summer, I lay out a salad bar with bowls of different ingredients and a choice of dressings so that everyone can help themselves. The Dressing for Dinner sauce (opposite) is my favourite and is particularly popular with my children. Here are some ideas for your salad bar.

A variety of different lettuces
Cherry tomatoes
Cucumber
Grated carrots
Sweet peppers
Tiny florets of broccoli or cauliflower
Cooked French beans
Cooked sweetcorn
Hard-boiled egg
Toasted sunflower seeds
Avocado tossed in lemon juice
Pine nuts
Tuna fish
Grated cheese or chopped blue cheese
Cooked pasta
Chopped chicken or turkey

Soy Sauce Dressing
15 ml (1 tbsp) balsamic or wine vinegar
a good pinch of dried mustard
a pinch of caster sugar
15 ml (1 tbsp) soy sauce
freshly ground black pepper
60 ml (4 tbsp) light olive oil

> **MENU PLANNING**
> *The perfect outdoor summer lunch – especially with a choice of dressings.*
> *See Summer Planner, page 12.*

To make the dressing, mix together the first five ingredients, then whisk in the olive oil.

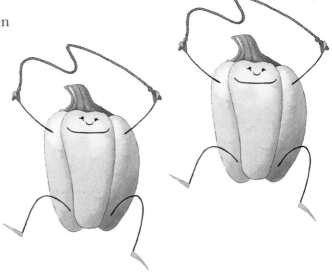

The Salad Bar with Soy Sauce Dressing is shown overleaf

Japanese Salad Dressing

This dressing is pure magic, and I can't make enough of it to please my children. It is based on the salad dressing served at a chain of popular American Japanese restaurants called Benihana. I use it to dress a mixed salad comprising crisp mixed lettuce, tomatoes, grated carrot, cucumber and sometimes thinly sliced radish. Once you've tried this recipe you will probably want to increase the quantities and keep a bottleful in your fridge.

Makes 6 portions

15 ml (1 tbsp) soy sauce
60 ml (4 tbsp) light crème fraîche
½ teaspoon minced or finely chopped ginger root

2 teaspoons caster sugar
30 ml (2 tbsp) rice wine vinegar

Combine the soy sauce, crème fraîche, ginger, caster sugar and vinegar with an electric hand-held blender and blend until smooth.

Dressing for Dinner

The secret of getting your child to enjoy eating salad is to make a seductive salad dressing. My children are all hooked on this Dressing for Dinner sauce and now prefer to come home to a plate of delicious salad vegetables than a bag of crisps and a chocolate biscuit.

Serves 5

25 g (1 oz) finely chopped onion
50 ml (2 fl oz) vegetable oil
30 ml (2 tbsp) rice wine vinegar
30 ml (2 tbsp) water
½ tablespoon chopped fresh ginger root
1 tablespoon chopped celery

15 ml (1 tbsp) soy sauce
7.5 ml (1½ tsp) tomato purée
7.5 ml (1½ tsp) sugar
5 ml (1 tsp) lemon juice
salt and freshly ground black pepper

Combine all the ingredients, except for the salt and pepper, in a blender or food processor and process until smooth. Season to taste.

TIP
Dressing for Dinner is also good mixed with a pasta salad comprising cooked pasta shapes, steamed cauliflower, French beans, sweetcorn, diced tomato and some diced, cooked chicken. It also makes an excellent salad for your child's lunchbox.

Bagel Snake

This is a fun way of arranging sandwiches and I find that bagels are popular with both children and their mums and dads. You can make the snake as long as you like depending on how many bagels you use and you can use a variety of toppings. I have chosen tuna and egg toppings, which are both nutritious, but, of course, there is an infinite variety of ingredients that you could choose, such as cream cheese and cucumber.

Serves 2

2 bagels

Tuna and cheese topping
1 x 185g (6 ½ oz) can of tuna in sunflower oil
(drained)
50 g (2 oz) Cheddar cheese, grated
45 ml (3 tbsp) mayonnaise
2 spring onions, finely sliced
salt and freshly ground black pepper

Egg mayonnaise with salad cress
2 to 3 hard-boiled eggs (10 minutes)
45 ml (3 tbsp) mayonnaise
1 tablespoon chives
3 tablespoons salad cress
salt and freshly ground black pepper

Decoration
a strip of red pepper
one stuffed olive, sliced
cherry tomatoes, halved
chives

Slice the bagels in half and then cut each half down the centre to form a semi-circle. Cut out the head of the snake from one of the pieces of bagel and the tail from another. Mix the ingredients for the tuna topping and mix the ingredients for the egg topping. Spread half the bagels with tuna and half with egg.

Decorate the tuna topping with halved cherry tomatoes and the egg topping with strips of chives arranged in a criss-cross pattern. Arrange the bagels to form the body of a snake. Then attach the head to the snake's body and arrange two slices of stuffed olive to form the eyes and cut out a forked tongue from the strip of red pepper.

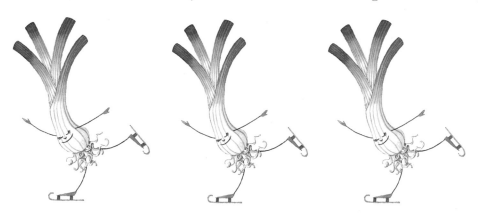

NOVELTY SHAPED SANDWICHES
Use cookie cutters to cut sandwiches into shapes like animals or gingerbread people. This really is a very simple way of transforming a simple sandwich into something special for your child. It can also be a particularly good way of tempting the reluctant sandwich eater, especially as the crusts tend to be removed.

Cheesy Pretzels

These make good snacks and children will have great fun twisting them into different shapes.

Makes 12 to 14 pretzels

200 g (7 oz) plain flour
25 g (1 oz) Cheddar cheese, grated
25 g (1 oz) butter, diced
2 teaspoons baking powder
1 teaspoon sugar
½ teaspoon salt
100 ml (3 fl oz) milk
1 egg, beaten

Toppings
coarse sea salt
sesame seeds
extra grated cheese

Pre-heat the oven to 200°C/400°F/Gas 6. Put the flour, cheese, butter, baking powder, sugar and salt in a mixing bowl and mix together with your fingers. Gradually add the milk to form a ball of dough. Sprinkle a clean surface with some flour and roll the dough around 3 or 4 times. Knead the dough by folding, pressing and turning and repeat this about 10 times.

Roll out the dough to a rectangle measuring about 25 x 18 cm (10 x 7 in). Cut the dough lengthways into strips each about 12 mm (½ in) wide. Pinch the edges and twist each strip into a pretzel shape. Put on a greased baking sheet, brush with beaten egg and sprinkle with coarse salt and sesame seeds or some extra grated cheese. Bake for 10 to 12 minutes or until golden.

A BALANCED LUNCHBOX
A packed lunch should contain:
✓ A high carbohydrate food, such as sandwiches or pasta salad
✓ Some protein, such as cheese, chicken drumstick or tuna
✓ Fresh fruit
✓ Something sweet and nutritious, such as a muffin, cereal bar or chocolate biscuit bar snack
✓ A drink, such as pure fruit juice, milk or milkshake.

Try to choose plenty of fresh foods, not too many highly refined foods.

Pasta

Annabel's 15-minute Tomato Sauce

There are now lots of wonderful ingredients available in most supermarkets like pesto and fresh basil, which can transform an ordinary tomato sauce into something very special. Vary the sauce by adding some sliced sautéed mushrooms.

Makes 4 portions

225 g (8 oz) spaghettini
30 ml (2 tbsp) olive oil
1 small onion, finely chopped
1 clove garlic, crushed
¼ to ½ teaspoon finely chopped red chilli
(optional)
2 x 400 g (14 oz) can of chopped tomatoes
30 ml (2 tbsp) red pesto
5 ml (1 tsp) balsamic vinegar
1 teaspoon caster sugar

salt and freshly ground black pepper
1 tablespoon fresh basil, torn into pieces
25 g (1 oz) Parmesan cheese, grated

> **MENU PLANNING**
> *Freeze family-sized quantities and you have
> an instant meal at any time.
> See Summer and Autumn Planners, pages
> 12 and 14.*

Cook the spaghettini according to the instructions on the packet. Sauté the onion, garlic and chilli, if using, in the olive oil for about 5 minutes. Drain the juice from one of the cans of tomatoes and stir in the drained tomatoes and the second can of tomatoes and juice and all the other ingredients except the basil and Parmesan cheese and let simmer for 10 minutes. Stir in the basil and Parmesan cheese until melted.

Lara's Lasagne

This is one of my daughter Lara's favourite dishes and in winter it makes a good family meal and freezes well. Lasagne seems to be one of those dishes that is popular with most children it provides a good source of iron and calcium.

Makes 6 portions

1 onion, chopped
1 clove garlic, crushed
½ red pepper, cored, de-seeded and chopped
15 ml (1 tbsp) olive oil
450 g (1 lb) lean minced beef
½ teaspoon mixed freeze-dried herbs
1 x 400 g (14 oz) can of chopped tomatoes,
drained
1 x 295 g (10 oz) can of condensed cream of
tomato soup
salt and freshly grated black pepper

Cheese sauce
50 g (2 oz) butter
40 g (1½ oz) flour
460 ml (16 fl oz) milk
a generous pinch of ground nutmeg
50 g (2 oz) Gruyère cheese, grated
25 g (1 oz) Parmesan cheese, grated

9 sheets fresh or no pre-cook lasagne

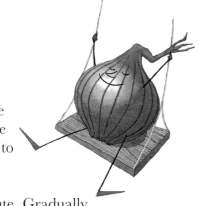

Pre-heat the oven to 190°C/375°F/Gas 5. Heat the oil in a large saucepan and sauté the onion, garlic and red pepper until softened. Add the beef and the herbs and sauté until the beef has changed colour. Add the remaining ingredients and cook over a medium heat for 15 to 20 minutes. Season to taste.

Meanwhile, to prepare the cheese sauce, melt the butter, stir in the flour and cook for 1 minute. Gradually whisk in the milk, bring to the boil and whisk until thickened and smooth. Season with the nutmeg and a little salt and pepper. Remove from the heat and stir in the grated Gruyère cheese until melted.

To assemble the lasagne, spoon a little of the meat sauce on to the base of an oven-proof dish 28 x 17 x 7 cm (11 x 6½ x 2¾ in). Cover with three sheets of lasagne. Divide the remaining meat sauce in half and cover the lasagne with half of the sauce. Spoon over a little of the cheese sauce.

Cover with three more sheets of lasagne and cover with the remaining meat sauce. Again spoon over a little of the cheese sauce but make sure that enough remains to completely cover the top layer of lasagne. Arrange the remaining sheets of lasagne on top and then spread over the remaining cheese sauce so that the lasagne is completely covered. Sprinkle over the Parmesan cheese and cook in the oven for 25 to 30 minutes.

Simon's Simple Pasta

This recipe was given to me by a barrister friend of mine, Simon Draycott, who having spent a long time staying in a hotel working on a case had a craving to eat this dish one night and phoned down to the kitchen with the instructions! The chef liked it so much that the recipe is now featured on the hotel's menu.

Makes 2 individual pizzas

1 onion, finely chopped
1 clove garlic, finely chopped
15 g (½ oz) butter
tagliatelle

100 g (4 oz) cured bacon, chopped
100 g (4 oz) button mushrooms, chopped
150 ml (¼ pint) crème fraîche

Melt the butter in a frying pan and sauté the onion, garlic and bacon over a low heat until soft (about 15 minutes), stirring occasionally. Meanwhile, cook the tagliatelle in a large pan of lightly salted water according to the instructions on the packet. Drain the pasta in a colander and pour over some boiling water to wash away the starch and prevent the pasta from sticking together.

Stir the mushrooms into the onion and bacon mixture and sauté for 5 minutes. Stir in the crème fraîche, season to taste and heat through. Remove from the heat and stir in the cooked tagliatelle.

Orient Express

Stir-fries are easy and quick to prepare as everything is cooked in the same pan, and they make a great family meal. As a short cut you can buy a ready prepared selection of stir-fry vegetables from your local supermarket. This can also be made with 300 g (10 oz) of beef cut into strips instead of the chicken. If you have some large carrots, it's fun to cut the carrot slices into stars using mini cookie cutters. Serve with rice or noodles. For extra appeal, how about using some 'child friendly' chopsticks made from brightly coloured plastic which are joined at the top.

Makes 6 portions

2 chicken breasts cut into strips

Marinade
15 ml (1 tbsp) soy sauce
15 ml (1 tbsp) sake or sherry
5 ml (1 tsp) sesame oil
1 teaspoon cornflour

225 g (8 oz) pasta twirls
45 ml (3 tbsp) vegetable oil
2 eggs, lightly beaten
1 onion, finely sliced
1 clove garlic, chopped (optional)
100 g (4 oz) small broccoli florets
100 g (4 oz) baby corn, cut in half

50 g (2 oz) red pepper, cut into strips
100 g (4 oz) carrots, cut into stars or strips
75 g (3 oz) button mushrooms, sliced
2 tablespoons finely sliced spring onion
22.5-30 ml (1½-2 tbsp) oyster sauce
1 chicken stock cube dissolved in 6 tablespoons boiling water
freshly ground black pepper

> **MENU PLANNING**
> *Serve with a cheesecake and fruit for a delicious dinner.*
> *See Spring Planner, page 10.*

Mix together the ingredients for the marinade and marinate the chicken for about 30 minutes. Cook the pasta in a large pan of lightly salted water according to the packet instructions.

In a frying pan, heat 7.5 ml (½ tbsp) of the oil and fry the eggs until set. Cut into strips and set aside. Then heat 15 ml (1 tbsp) of the oil in a wok or large frying pan and stir-fry half the onion and garlic for about 2 to 3 minutes. Add the chicken and marinade, and stir-fry until the chicken is cooked through. Remove the chicken and onion and set aside.

Heat the remaining oil in the wok or frying pan and stir-fry the rest of the garlic and onion for 2 to 3 minutes. Add the broccoli, baby corn, red pepper and carrots and stir-fry for about 5 minutes. Sprinkle over a little water while stir-frying the vegetables. Add the mushrooms and spring onions and cook for 2 to 3 minutes.

Return the chicken to the wok, add the oyster sauce and stock and continue to cook for 2 to 3 minutes, or until the vegetables are tender and the chicken cooked through.

Easy Bolognese Sauce

This is a very quick and easy way to make a bolognese sauce using a can of tomato soup as one of the ingredients. Since red meat provides the best source of iron, it's good to find some family favourites that include it and this pasta sauce is particularly appealing to children.

Makes 4 adult or 8 child portions

1 large onion, chopped
1 clove garlic, crushed
15 ml (1 tbsp) vegetable oil
500 g (1 lb 2 oz) lean minced beef
½ teaspoon mixed freeze-dried herbs

100 g (4 oz) button mushrooms, sliced
1 x 400 g (14 oz) can of chopped tomatoes
1 x 295g (10 oz) can of condensed cream of tomato soup
400 g (14 oz) spaghetti

Sauté the onion and garlic in the oil for 2 to 3 minutes. Add the beef and the herbs and sauté until the beef has changed colour. Add the sliced mushrooms and sauté for 2 minutes. Add the remaining ingredients and cook over a medium heat for about 15 minutes. Season to taste. Meanwhile, cook the spaghetti in a large pan of lightly salted water according to the instructions on the packet. Mix the cooked pasta with the bolognese sauce and serve.

Three-cheese Macaroni

Pasta provides a good source of complex carbohydrate so this macaroni will boost your child's energy level as well as providing a good source of protein and calcium. For a meaty variation, add some chopped bacon.

Makes 4 portions

300g (11 oz) short macaroni
25 g (1 oz) butter
25 g (1 oz) plain flour
1 teaspoon English mustard powder
600 ml (1 pint) milk

100 g (4 oz) Cheddar cheese, grated
50 g (2 oz) Gruyère cheese, grated
25 g (1 oz) Parmesan cheese, grated
salt and freshly ground black pepper

Cook the macaroni in a large saucepan of lightly salted water according to the instructions on the packet. Drain thoroughly. Melt the butter in a pan, stir in the flour and mustard powder and cook, stirring, for 30 seconds. Gradually whisk in the milk, bring to the boil and then simmer for a few minutes to make a smooth sauce.

Stir in 75 g (3 oz) of the Cheddar cheese and all the Gruyère and Parmesan cheese until melted. Season to taste. Transfer to an oven-proof dish, top with the extra Cheddar cheese and place under a pre-heated grill until the top is golden.

Lasagne with Spinach, Cheese and Tomato

This is my favourite vegetarian lasagne. If you can find sheets of fresh lasagne, I think they taste better than dried, and some supermarkets stock them in the chilled cabinet. If using the dried lasagne, you may need to cook this for 5 minutes longer and make sure that the lasagne is completely covered with sauce or it will dry out.

Makes 4 portions

Tomato sauce
1 onion, chopped
1 clove garlic, crushed
15 ml (1 tbsp) olive oil
30 ml (2 tbsp) tomato purée
2 x 400 g (14 oz) cans of chopped tomatoes
1 tablespoon fresh chopped parsley
1 tablespoon torn basil leaves
1 teaspoon dried oregano
½ teaspoon sugar
salt and freshly ground black pepper
225g (8 oz) frozen or 450g (1 lb) fresh spinach
15 g (½ oz) butter
175 g (6 oz) cottage cheese

1 egg, lightly beaten
30 ml (2 tbsp) double cream
25 g (1 oz) Parmesan cheese, grated
15 g (½ oz) Gruyère cheese, grated
6 sheets fresh lasagne or dried no pre-cook lasagne
125 g (4½ oz) Mozzarella cheese, grated

> **MENU PLANNING**
> *On a cool evening serve with a warm blackberry and apple pudding.*
> *See Autumn Planner, page 14.*

Pre-heat the oven to 180°C/350°F/Gas 4. To make the tomato sauce, sauté the onion and garlic in the olive oil until softened. Add the tomato purée and sauté for 1 minute. Drain and discard the juice from the cans of tomatoes and add the tomatoes to the sautéed onions. Add all the remaining ingredients and simmer uncovered for 10 minutes. Season to taste.

Meanwhile, to prepare the spinach and cheese layer, cook the spinach, drain thoroughly and then sauté in the butter for a couple of minutes. In a food processor, blend together the spinach, cottage cheese, egg, double cream and Parmesan cheese. Season with a little black pepper.

To assemble the lasagne, spread a thin layer of the tomato sauce over the base of a fairly deep oven-proof dish measuring about 23 x 15 cm (9 x 6 in). Lay two sheets of lasagne on top. Cover with half the spinach mixture, a third of the Mozzarella cheese and a third of the tomato sauce. Again, lay two sheets of lasagne on top, spoon the remaining spinach mixture on top and then cover with a third of the Mozzarella cheese and a third of the tomato sauce.

Lay the remaining two sheets of lasagne on top, cover with the remaining tomato sauce and Mozzarella cheese and then sprinkle the extra Parmesan or Gruyère cheese over the top. Bake in the oven for about 25 minutes.

Linguine with Spring Vegetables

Since pasta is generally so popular with children it's a good idea to combine it with foods that they are not so keen on eating. Here I have chosen some brightly coloured diced vegetables to make a delicious sauce for linguine or spaghetti.

Makes 4 portions

350 g (12 oz) linguine
30 ml (2 tbsp) vegetable oil
1 onion, finely chopped
3 fresh tomatoes, peeled, de-seeded and chopped
175 g (6 oz) carrots, finely diced
225 g (8 oz) courgettes, finely diced
175 g (6 oz) red pepper, cored, de-seeded and finely diced
2 spring onions, finely sliced

1 chicken stock cube dissolved in 250 ml (8 fl oz) boiling water
22.5 ml (1½ tbsp) soy sauce
salt and freshly ground black pepper

MENU PLANNING
Just the thing for a light lunch.
See Spring Planner, page 10.

Cook the linguine in a large pan of lightly salted boiling water according to the instructions on the packet. Drain and set aside. Heat the oil in a wok or frying pan and sauté the onion for 3 minutes. Add the tomatoes and sauté for 2 minutes. Add the carrots, sauté for 2 minutes stirring occasionally, then stir-fry the courgettes, red peppers and spring onions for 4 minutes. Pour in the chicken stock and soy sauce, cover the pan and cook for 6 minutes. Add the cooked linguine and heat through for about 2 minutes. Season to taste and serve with plenty of freshly grated Parmesan cheese.

Bow-tie Pasta with Peas and Prosciutto

Here is a simple and quick pasta dish that tends to be popular with young children. You could also add a little crème fraiche or double cream to the sauce if you like. The garlic is optional in this dish because it is especially pronounced; if you or your children aren't too keen on garlic, feel free to omit it.

Makes 2 portions

15 ml (1 tbsp) olive oil
25 g (1 oz) butter
1 onion, finely chopped
1 clove garlic, crushed
75 g (3 oz) frozen peas
1 tablespoon chopped fresh parsley

125 ml (4 fl oz) chicken stock (see Chicken Soup on page 47)
40 g (1½ oz) prosciutto, finely diced
200 g (7 oz) bow-tie pasta
2 tablespoons freshly grated Parmesan cheese

Heat the olive oil and a small knob of the butter and sauté the onion and garlic (if using) for about 8 minutes or until softened. Add the peas, cook for 1 minute, then stir in the parsley and chicken stock. Bring to the boil, then reduce the heat and cook for 4 to 5 minutes. Stir in the prosciutto.

Meanwhile, cook the pasta in a large pan of lightly salted water according to the instructions on the packet. Drain the pasta, return to the warm pan, add the remaining butter and toss until it melts. Stir in the grated Parmesan cheese. Re-heat the peas and prosciutto and toss with the cooked pasta. Serve with some extra freshly grated Parmesan cheese if you wish.

Penne with Chicken, Tomatoes and Basil

There is a lovely mixture of flavours in this tasty chicken and pasta dish and it's very quick and easy to put together.

Makes 4 portions

200 g (7 oz) penne pasta
15 ml (1 tbsp) olive oil
a knob of butter
2 shallots or 1 small onion, finely chopped
25 g (1 oz) pine kernels
2 boneless chicken breasts, thinly sliced into strips
50 g (2 oz) sun-dried tomatoes, drained and sliced
150 ml (¼ pint) chicken stock (see Chicken Soup on page 47)

150 ml (¼ pint) crème fraîche
25 g (1 oz) Parmesan cheese, grated
salt and freshly ground black pepper
2 tablespoons shredded basil leaves

> **MENU PLANNING**
> *Precede with soup and follow with crumble – warming and nourishing.*
> *See Autumn Planner, page 14*

Cook the pasta in a large pan of lightly salted water according to the instructions on the packet, drain and set aside. Meanwhile, heat the oil and butter in a large frying pan and sauté the shallots or onion and pine kernels for about 5 minutes, stirring occasionally. Add the strips of chicken and sauté, stirring occasionally, for about 6 minutes. Add the sun-dried tomatoes and cook for 1 minute.

Pour the chicken stock into the frying pan and bring to the boil. Stir in the crème fraîche and Parmesan cheese and season with a little salt and freshly ground black pepper. Drain the pasta, toss with the sauce and stir in the fresh basil.

PRESERVING VITAMIN CONTENT

Many commercially frozen vegetables and fruits, such as peas, spinach, sweetcorn and berry fruits are frozen within 2 to 3 hours of being picked, thus ensuring that they retain their vital nutrients. In fact, fresh vegetables and fruits that have been stored for several days can sometimes contain fewer nutrients than the frozen variety.

The best method of cooking to retain maximum nutrients is steaming, microwaving or stir-frying. Boiled broccoli retains only 35% of its vitamin C as opposed to 72% when it is steamed or microwaved. If you want to boil vegetables, cook them in a small amount of water (just enough to cover the vegetables) and do not overcook. Scrub or wash fruit and vegetables rather than peeling them, as most of the nutrients lie just beneath the surface. When possible, try to buy organic fruit and vegetables. Vitamin C dissolves in water so avoid standing fruit and vegetables in water.

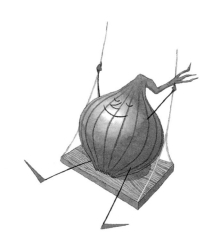

Vegetable Tagliatelle

This is a lovely light sauce with vegetables, cherry tomatoes and shredded gem lettuce, which can be served with almost any kind of pasta. It is a particularly good summer pasta recipe.

Makes 4 portions

200 g (7 oz) tagliatelle
15 ml (1 tbsp) olive oil
1 onion, finely chopped
1 clove garlic, finely chopped
1 small yellow pepper, cut into strips
1 medium courgette, sliced diagonally and cut
into semi-circles

125 ml (4 fl oz) light crème fraîche
125 ml (4 fl oz) vegetable stock
8 cherry tomatoes, halved
½ baby gem lettuce, shredded
75g (3 oz) Parmesan cheese, grated
salt and freshly ground black pepper

Cook the tagliatelle in a large pan of lightly salted boiling water according to the directions on the packet. Heat the olive oil in a heavy-bottomed saucepan and sauté the onion and garlic for 1 minute. Add the yellow pepper and courgette and sauté for about 8 minutes or until tender. Stir in the crème fraîche and the vegetable stock and bring to a simmer. Stir in the cherry tomatoes and simmer for 1 minute. Add the shredded lettuce and Parmesan cheese and season to taste. Toss the drained tagliatelle with the sauce. Serve with extra Parmesan cheese to sprinkle on top if you wish.

Turkey Bolognese

A tasty, quick and easy sauce for pasta. You could also make this using minced chicken.

Makes 4 portions

1 large onion, finely chopped
1 clove garlic, finely chopped
1 small red pepper, finely diced
30 ml (2 tbsp) vegetable oil
500 g (1 lb 2 oz) minced turkey
1 medium carrot, peeled and grated
1 x 400 g (14 oz) can of chopped tomatoes

1 chicken stock cube dissolved in 150 ml
(¼ pint) boiling water
15 ml (1 tbsp) Tomato Ketchup
1 tbsp fresh sage or ½ tsp dried sage
½ tbsp fresh thyme leaves or ¼ tsp dried thyme
salt and freshly ground black pepper
350 g (12 oz) spaghetti or penne

Sauté the onion, garlic and red pepper in the vegetable oil for 3 to 4 minutes. Add the turkey mince and stir until it changes colour, breaking up any lumps with a fork. Add the remaining ingredients, bring to the boil and then simmer uncovered, stirring occasionally, for 30 minutes. Meanwhile, cook the pasta according to the instructions on the packet, drain and toss with the sauce.

Tagliatelle with Prawns and Vegetables

I often make this for my own supper as two of my favourite foods are pasta and prawns. It also makes an excellent vegetable pasta dish without the prawns.

Makes 4 portions

200 g (7 oz) tagliatelle
a knob of butter
425 ml (¾ pint) chicken stock (see Chicken
Soup on page 47)
5 ml (1 tsp) lemon juice
175 g (6 oz) cauliflower, cut into small florets
1 medium carrot, cut into matchsticks
50 g (2 oz) French beans or mangetout,
trimmed
25 g (1 oz) butter
1 small onion, finely chopped
1 small garlic clove, crushed
100 g (4 oz) small courgettes, cut into
matchsticks

175 g (6 oz) cooked and peeled king prawns
either fresh or frozen and defrosted
1 tablespoon chopped fresh parsley
salt and freshly ground black pepper
1 tablespoon cornflour
60 ml (4 tbsp) light crème fraîche
25 g (1 oz) Parmesan cheese, grated

> **MENU PLANNING**
> *Ice cream and fruit make the perfect summer*
> *dessert.*
> *See Summer Planner, page 12.*

Cook the tagliatelle in a large saucepan of lightly salted water according to the instructions on the packet. When it is just tender, drain, add the knob of butter and toss the warm pasta with the butter. Set aside.

Put the chicken stock and lemon juice into a saucepan, bring to the boil, add the cauliflower, carrots and French beans or mangetout and cook over a medium heat for about 6 minutes or until the vegetables are just tender. Strain the vegetables, reserving the stock for later use.

Melt the butter in a frying pan, add the onion and garlic and sauté for 3 to 4 minutes. Add the courgettes and continue to cook for 3 to 4 minutes. Cut the prawns in half and add together with the parsley and the drained vegetables, lightly season and cook for 2 to 3 minutes or until heated through.

Mix a little of the reserved stock with the cornflour and heat the remaining stock in a saucepan. Mix the cornflour liquid into the remaining stock and cook, stirring for about 3 minutes or until the sauce thickens. Remove from the heat and stir in the crème fraîche. Toss the tagliatelle with the vegetables and sauce until well mixed. Serve with grated Parmesan cheese.

Scarlett's Pasta

This pasta dish is a great favourite with my children, especially Scarlett, who loves both pasta and salami. You could also use sliced sausage instead of salami if you prefer.

Makes 4 portions

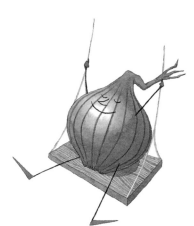

2 shallots, finely chopped
½ small red pepper, chopped
15 ml (1 tbsp) olive oil
1 x 400 g (14 oz) can of chopped tomatoes, drained
180 ml (6 fl oz) strong chicken stock (see Chicken Soup on page 47)
225 g (8 oz) pasta
1 tablespoon fresh basil, shredded

1 tablespoon Parmesan cheese, grated
100 g (4 oz) salami, cut into strips
salt and freshly ground black pepper

MENU PLANNING
Pasta is so quick to prepare that it is great for lunchtime.
See Autumn Planner, page 14.

Sauté the shallots and red pepper in the olive oil for about 5 minutes or until softened. Stir in the tomatoes and sauté for 2 minutes, then add the stock and simmer for about 10 minutes. Meanwhile, cook the pasta according to the instructions on the packet. When cooked, stir in the basil, Parmesan cheese and salami, heat through and season to taste. Drain the pasta and toss with the sauce.

VERY QUICK AND EASY PASTA SAUCE

For a simple sauce that tastes delicious, simmer 300 ml (½ pint) single cream with 50 g (2 oz) butter and seasoning. Toss with freshly cooked pasta like tagliatelle and fresh Parmesan cheese.

Poultry

Chicken Balls in Sweet and Sour Sauce

The grated apple adds a delicious flavour to these chicken balls which makes them appealing to children. They also make good finger food on their own. Alternatively, use minced meat to make meatballs in sweet and sour sauce.

Makes 4 portions

2 large chicken breasts, cut into chunks
1 onion, finely chopped
1 tbsp parsley
50 g (2 oz) fresh white breadcrumbs
1 large Granny Smith apple, peeled and grated
10 ml (2 tsp) chicken stock, dissolved in 5 ml
(1 tsp) boiling water
flour for coating
vegetable oil for frying

Sweet and sour sauce
1 onion, finely chopped
1 small red pepper, de-seeded and chopped
22.5 ml (1½ tbsp) vegetable oil
1 x 400 g (14 oz) can of chopped tomatoes
15 ml (1 tbsp) tomato purée
150 ml (5 fl oz) pineapple juice
5 ml (1 tsp) brown sugar
5 ml (1 tsp) malt vinegar
5 ml (1 tsp) soy sauce

Using your hands, squeeze out some of the excess liquid from the grated apple. Mix together the chicken, onion, parsley, breadcrumbs, grated apple and chicken stock and chop in a food processor for a few seconds. Season with a little salt and pepper. With your hands, form into about 20 balls, roll in flour and fry in shallow oil until lightly golden (about 10 minutes). For the sauce, sauté the onion and sweet pepper in the oil until softened. Add the rest of the ingredients, plus freshly ground black pepper, bring to the boil and simmer, covered, for 15 minutes. Pour over the balls and serve with rice.

Sasha's Chicken

Sasha is a Russian friend of mine and a wonderful cook. She has a lovely little boy Daniel, who is 2 years old and who my two daughters love to play with – and pretend that they are little mummys. This is a recipe handed down to Sasha by her grandmother, who used to dry tomatoes on the roof of her summer house in the Ukraine.

Makes 4 portions

25 g (1 oz) butter
50 g (2 oz) sun-dried tomatoes (in oil)
8 basil leaves
a squeeze of lemon juice

150 ml (¼ pint) single cream
4 chicken breasts, cut into strips
125 ml (4 fl oz) water
salt and freshly ground black pepper

Pre-heat the oven to 180°C/350°F/Gas 4. Put the butter, chopped sun-dried tomatoes, basil leaves, lemon juice and 60 ml (4 tbsp) of the cream into a food processor and mix on pulse setting for a few seconds. Season the strips of chicken and put them in a shallow oven-proof dish. Mix together the sun-dried tomato mixture, the rest of the cream and the water, lightly season and pour this over the chicken to cover. Cook in the oven for 30 minutes uncovered.

Annabel's Tasty Chicken Skewers

These skewers can also be interspersed with some vegetables, such as chunks of red pepper, onion or some button mushrooms. Brush the vegetables with the marinade before cooking the skewers. Alternatively, make skewers with chicken only and serve with boiled rice and stir-fry chopped onion and diced red and yellow peppers in some olive oil and stir into the cooked rice to give it both colour and flavour.

Makes 4 portions

4 chicken breasts cut into chunks
60 ml (4 tbsp) soy sauce
40 g (1½ oz) light muscovado sugar
15 ml (1 tbsp) lime or lemon juice
15 ml (1 tbsp) vegetable oil
1 clove garlic, crushed

> **MENU PLANNING**
> *Use either of the recipes on this page to accompany a barbecue.*
> *See Summer Planner, page 12.*

Put the soy sauce and sugar into a small saucepan and gently heat, stirring until the sugar has dissolved. Remove from the heat, stir in the lime juice, vegetable oil and garlic. Marinate the chicken for at least 1 hour or overnight. Soak 8 bamboo skewers in water to prevent them from getting scorched. Pre-heat the oven to 180°C/350°F/Gas 4. Thread the chunks of chicken on to the skewers and cook in the oven for 4 to 5 minutes each side, basting occasionally with the marinade until cooked through.

Teriyaki Chicken Skewers

Marinated chicken skewers make an easy to prepare and very tasty meal. They can also be cooked on a barbecue.

Makes 4 portions

4 chicken breasts

Marinade
30 ml (2 tbsp) soy sauce
30 ml (2 tbsp) sesame oil

30 ml (2 tbsp) rice wine vinegar
1 tablespoon sugar
1 spring onion, thinly sliced
1 garlic clove, chopped
¼ teaspoon grated ginger root

Combine the ingredients for the marinade. Cut the chicken into 2.5 cm (1 in) cubes and marinate for at least 1 hour. Soak eight bamboo skewers in water for 30 minutes to prevent them from scorching. Pre-heat the oven to 200°C/400°F/Gas 6. Thread the pieces of chicken on to the skewers. Then place the skewers in a pan lined with foil and pour over the marinade. Bake for about 7 minutes. Turn over and brush with the sauce and bake for 4-5 minutes on each side more or until the chicken is cooked through.

The Teriyaki Chicken Skewers are shown overleaf

Chicken Piccata

Here are tender breasts of chicken cooked in a delicious, quick and easy to prepare Chinese-style sauce.

Makes 2 portions

2 boneless chicken breasts

Marinade
15 ml (1 tbsp) lemon juice
15 ml (1 tbsp) water
1 tablespoon finely chopped onion

plain flour
salt and freshly ground black pepper
30 ml (2 tbsp) vegetable oil

Sauce
250 ml (8 fl oz) chicken stock (see Chicken
Soup on page 47)
10 ml (2 tsp) soy sauce
5 ml (1 tsp) sesame oil
1 tablespoon sugar
1 teaspoon cider vinegar
1 tablespoon cornflour
ground white pepper
1 spring onion, thinly sliced

Rinse the chicken and pat dry with paper towels. Place the chicken breasts under a layer of plastic wrap. Using the flat side of a meat mallet, pound until quite thin and cut each breast in half. Remove the plastic wrap and place the chicken in a shallow dish. Mix together the lemon juice and water, add the chopped onion and marinate the chicken in this for 30 minutes. Remove the chicken pieces and discard the marinade. Dip the chicken in seasoned flour. Heat the vegetable oil in a frying pan or wok and sauté the chicken for about 5 minutes on each side or until lightly browned and cooked through. Meanwhile, put all the ingredients for the sauce into a saucepan and bring to the boil. Cook over a medium heat, stirring until thickened. Drain away any excess oil from the pan in which the chicken was cooked, pour the sauce over the cooked chicken and heat through.

Creamy Chicken with Vegetables

Tender succulent pieces of chicken are quickly cooked with fresh vegetables in a creamy sauce flavoured with a little white wine and lemon juice. This is good served on a bed of rice.

Serves 4

4 chicken breasts
25 g (1 oz) butter
15 ml (1 tbsp) vegetable oil
75 g (3 oz) baby carrots, cut into strips
75 g (3 oz) French beans
3 shallots, or 1 medium onion, finely chopped
100 g (4 oz) button mushrooms, sliced

1 tablespoon flour
50 ml (2 fl oz) dry white wine
250 ml (8 fl oz) chicken stock (see Chicken
Soup on page 47)
45 to 60 ml (3 to 4 tbsp) double cream
22.5 ml (1½ tbsp) fresh lemon juice
salt and freshly ground black pepper

Cut the chicken into bite-sized pieces and sauté in half the oil and butter until just cooked. Meanwhile, steam, microwave or boil the carrots and beans separately until tender but still crisp. Remove the chicken from the pan and set aside. Add the rest of the butter and oil to the pan and sauté the shallots or onion until softened. Add the mushrooms and sauté for 2 minutes. Sprinkle with the flour and cook for 1 minute.

Gradually add the wine and chicken stock, bring to the boil, stirring until thickened. Add the carrots and beans and simmer for 2 minutes. Mix in the cream and chicken and simmer for 5 minutes or until the chicken is cooked through. Stir in the lemon juice and season to taste.

Turkey Meatballs with Tomato Sauce

These turkey balls are also delicious served plain. The apple brings out the flavour and keeps the turkey balls moist.

Makes 24 turkey balls

2 medium apples, peeled and grated
450 g (1 lb) minced turkey
15 ml (1 tbsp) vegetable oil
100 g (4 oz) leek, finely chopped
50 g (2 oz) fresh white breadcrumbs
1 teaspoon finely chopped fresh thyme
or ½ teaspoon dried mixed herbs
1 tablespoon fresh parsley, finely chopped
1 chicken stock cube, crumbled
30 ml (2 tbsp) cold water
salt and freshly ground black pepper
30 ml (2 tbsp) vegetable oil for frying

Tomato sauce

1 small onion, finely chopped
1 clove garlic, finely chopped
30 ml (2 tbsp) olive oil
15 ml (1 tbsp) tomato purée
1 x 400 g (14 oz) can of chopped tomatoes
150 ml (¼ pint) chicken stock (see Chicken Soup on page 47)
5 ml (1 tsp) balsamic vinegar
¼ teaspoon sugar
2 tablespoons torn basil leaves
1 to 2 tablespoons grated Parmesan cheese

Squeeze out half the juice from the apple by pressing between your hands. Then sauté the leek in the vegetable oil for 3 to 4 minutes or until softened. Then combine all the ingredients in a large mixing bowl and season to taste. Using your hands, form the mixture into walnut-sized balls and sauté in the vegetable oil until golden.

To make the tomato sauce, sauté the onion and garlic in the olive oil until softened. Stir in the tomato purée and cook, stirring, for 1 minute. Add the chopped tomatoes, chicken stock, balsamic vinegar and sugar. Stir in the basil and Parmesan cheese and season to taste. Cook over a medium heat for 10 minutes. Add the turkey balls and continue to cook for 10 minutes more.

Turkey Burgers

These turkey burgers can also be eaten sandwiched between a bun and layered with salad and tomato sauce. Sometimes, children prefer these without herbs so you can leave them out of their portions. (*See photograph opposite*)

Makes 12 burgers

450 g (1 lb) turkey breast, roughly chopped, or minced turkey
1 onion, finely chopped
1 tablespoon fresh chopped thyme or oregano or ½ teaspoon dried
1 tablespoon fresh chopped parsley
1 apple, peeled and grated (squeeze out excess juice)

50 g (2 oz) fresh white breadcrumbs
5 ml (1 tsp) Worcestershire sauce
1 chicken stock cube dissolved in 22.5 ml (1½ tbsp) boiling water
50 g (2 oz) plain flour
2 eggs, lightly beaten
75 g (3 oz) fresh white breadcrumbs
vegetable oil for frying

Mix together the turkey, onion, herbs and apple. Chop for a few seconds in a food processor. Return the mixture to a large bowl and stir in the breadcrumbs, stock and Worcestershire sauce and season to taste. Using your hands, form the mixture into 12 burgers. Dip the burgers in the flour, then in the egg and coat with the breadcrumbs. Heat the vegetable oil in a frying pan and sauté the burgers for about 4 minutes on each side or until golden and cooked through.

Heavenly Barbecued Burgers

These tasty burgers can be made with chicken, beef or lamb – they are irresistible and children love them.

Makes 6 burgers

450 g (1 lb) chopped chicken, minced beef or lamb
1 medium onion, finely chopped
½ red pepper, cored, de-seeded and chopped
15 ml (1 tbsp) vegetable oil
2 tablespoons finely chopped fresh parsley
½ chicken stock cube, dissolved in 45 ml (3 tbsp) of boiling water

25 g (1 oz) breadcrumbs
1 Granny Smith apple, peeled and grated
salt and freshly ground black pepper

Sauce
30 ml (2 tbsp) Hoisin sauce
15 ml (1 tbsp) water
5 ml (1 tsp) sesame oil

Sauté the onion and red pepper until soft (about 10 minutes). Combine these with all the other ingredients and, using your hands, form into about 6 burgers. Mix together the sauce ingredients and brush the burgers with half the sauce. Place the burgers directly on the grill or use a hinged basket, which holds the food between two wire racks. Cook for about 5 minutes on one side. Turn, brush with the remaining sauce and barbecue for 8 to 10 minutes or until cooked through.

Fruity Curried Chicken

A mild, deliciously flavoured chicken curry. This is a recipe that my mother used to make for me when I was a child. I like a pretty tame curry but you can always make it more fiery by using a medium or hot curry powder. Serve with plain rice and poppadums.

Makes 6 portions

1 chicken cut into about 8 pieces
plain flour
salt and freshly ground black pepper
vegetable oil
2 medium onions, peeled and chopped
2 tablespoons mild curry powder
90 ml (6 tbsp) tomato purée
900 ml (1½ pints) chicken stock (see Chicken
Soup on page 47)
1 cooking apple (about 225 g/8 oz), peeled
and thinly sliced
1 large carrot, peeled and thinly sliced

2 lemon slices
75 g (3 oz) sultanas
1 bay leaf
1 dessertspoon brown sugar

> **MENU PLANNING**
> *Try combining various ethnic foods – this*
> *curry works well with Loshken Pudding*
> *or a Tiramisu*
> *See Autumn and Winter Planners, pages 14*
> *and 16.*

Pre-heat the oven to 180°C/350°F/Gas 4. Trim any fat from the chicken and remove some of the skin. Coat the chicken with seasoned flour. Fry in the vegetable oil until lightly golden, then drain on kitchen paper and place in a casserole dish. Heat 30 ml (2 tbsp) of vegetable oil in a frying pan and sauté the onion for about 10 minutes or until softened but not coloured. Stir in the curry powder and the tomato purée and continue to cook for 2 to 3 minutes. Stir in 2 tablespoons of flour and stir in 300 ml (½ pint) of the stock.

Add the sliced apple, carrot, lemon slices, sultanas, bay leaf, brown sugar and the rest of the stock. Season with salt and pepper. Pour the sauce over the chicken in the casserole, cover and cook in the oven for 1 hour. Remove the lemon slices and bay leaf, take the chicken off the bone and cut into pieces.

Chicken and Potato Pancake

These pancakes are deliciously thick, golden and crispy with a soft succulent centre. This recipe can be varied by adding other vegetables like grated courgettes or chopped sweet peppers. I make it in a 20 cm (8 in) frying pan and my children enjoy cutting their own slices – it can be eaten either hot or cold.

Makes 4 portions

1 chicken breast, cut into pieces, or 75 g (3 oz) left-over cooked chicken
300 ml (½ pint) chicken or vegetable stock (see Chicken Soup on page 47)
1 baking potato, peeled and grated
1 onion, peeled and grated

40 g (1½ oz) frozen peas
1 small egg, beaten
1 tablespoon flour
salt and freshly ground black pepper
30 ml (2 tbsp) vegetable oil

Poach the chicken breast in the stock until cooked through (10-15 minutes). Press out the liquid from the grated potato and combine the potato with the onion, frozen peas, egg and flour, and season lightly with some salt and freshly ground black pepper. Dice the chicken and add it to the vegetable mixture.

Heat 15 ml (1 tbsp) of the oil in a 20-cm (8-in) frying pan, tilt the pan so that the oil coats the sides, and press the mixture into the pan. Fry for about 5 minutes or until browned. Turn the pancake on to a plate. Heat the rest of the oil and brown the pancake on the other side for about 7 minutes. Cut into wedges and serve.

Finger Licking Chicken Drumsticks

Chicken drumsticks tend to be very popular with children and are good either hot or cold. This tasty marinade gives them a wonderful flavour and they can be prepared the day before, refrigerated and then wrapped in foil for your child's lunchbox. Always take care to cook chicken right through to avoid food poisoning.

Makes 4 portions

4 large drumsticks

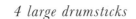

Marinade
22.5 ml (1½ tbsp) cider or white wine vinegar
60 ml (4 tbsp) tomato sauce
30 ml (2 tbsp) clear honey
7.5 ml ½ tbsp) mustard
7.5 ml (½ tbsp) Worcestershire sauce
7.5 ml (½ tbsp) vegetable oil

Mix all the ingredients for the marinade together in a bowl. Skin the drumsticks, make 2 or 3 slashes in the flesh and add to the marinade, turning a few times to make sure that they are well coated. Cover and refrigerate for at least 2 hours or overnight.

Pre-heat the oven to 220°C/425°F/Gas 7. Arrange the drumsticks in a shallow roasting tin and pour over the marinade. Cook for 35-40 minutes, or until cooked through, basting occasionally with the sauce.

Basket-weave Chicken Breasts

The bright orange and green basket-weave pattern made by the carrot and courgette strips looks sensational wrapped around these stuffed chicken breasts. They are surprisingly easy to make and children will love to help weave the vegetable strips together. If your child prefers, you can stuff the chicken breasts with some cheese and ham.

Makes 2 portions

2 large chicken breasts
1 large carrot
1 large courgette
1 shallot, finely chopped
75 g (3 oz) button mushrooms, chopped
7.5 ml (½ tbsp) vegetable oil and a knob of butter
1 teaspoon fresh chopped parsley
a squeeze of lemon juice
1 tablespoon breadcrumbs

salt and freshly ground black pepper

Tarragon sauce
60 ml (2 fl oz) chicken stock (see Chicken Soup on page 47)
22.5 ml (1½ tbsp) lime or lemon juice
50 g (2 oz) cold butter, cut into cubes
½ tablespoon chopped tarragon
30 ml (2 tbsp) double cream

Using a potato peeler, cut the carrot and courgette lengthways into long thin strips. Blanch them in boiling water for just under 1 minute and place on absorbent kitchen paper to dry.

To prepare the mushroom stuffing, sauté the shallot in the butter and oil until softened, add the chopped mushrooms and cook for 3 to 4 minutes. Add the parsley, lemon juice and breadcrumbs and cook for 2 minutes. Season to taste. Cut a slit in each of the chicken breasts to form a pocket and stuff with the mushroom mixture. Season the chicken.

Place five strips of courgette horizontally quite close together on top of a piece of plastic food wrap (suitable for cooking) just big enough to wrap around the chicken breast. Weave five strips of carrot vertically through the courgette strips to make a basket-weave pattern. Wrap the plastic food wrap and woven vegetables around the chicken breasts to form a parcel. Cook in a steamer for about 20 minutes or until cooked through.

To make the sauce, put the stock and lime or lemon juice in a small saucepan and bring to the boil. Remove from the heat and whisk in the butter. Stir in the tarragon and cream and season to taste. Pour some of the sauce on to a plate, remove the plastic food wrap and place the chicken breasts on top of the sauce.

Chicken Burgers with Courgette and Apple

The grated apples and courgettes give these burgers a lovely moist flavour. They are a great favourite with the whole family and also make a good standby in the freezer.
They are good served in a bun with salad and tomato sauce or simply with baked beans.

Makes 12 burgers

2 breasts of chicken, minced
1 tablespoon fresh chopped parsley
1 onion, finely chopped
2 apples, grated
225 g (8 oz) courgettes, grated
1 chicken stock cube, crumbled

salt and freshly ground black pepper
100 g (4 oz) flour
2 eggs, lightly beaten
150 g (5 oz) breadcrumbs
vegetable oil for frying

Put the chicken, parsley and onion into a food processor and chop for a few seconds on pulse. Squeeze the excess moisture from the apples and courgettes, and mix these into the chicken together with the crumbled stock cube and a little salt and freshly ground black pepper. Using your hands, form into burgers. Coat in flour, then in the beaten egg and then coat with the breadcrumbs. Heat the oil in a large frying pan and sauté the burgers until golden, taking about 6 minutes on each side.

Terrific Turkey Schnitzels

These turkey schnitzels are a great favourite and quick to cook. I like to serve them with spaghettini (very thin spaghetti) and tomato sauce, preferably home-made (see page 64). If you can't find turkey fillets you could substitute chicken breasts pounded quite thin. If you don't have sesame seeds, use 65 g (2½ oz) breadcrumbs instead. It will improve the flavour if you marinate the turkey in lemon juice and garlic before coating with the breadcrumbs and sesame seeds.

Makes 2 portions

2 turkey fillets (about 175 g / 6 oz each)

Marinade
15 ml (1 tbsp) olive oil
30 ml (2 tbsp) lemon juice
1 small clove garlic, thinly sliced

plain flour
salt and freshly ground black pepper
1 egg

15 ml (1 tbsp) milk
50 g (2 oz) breadcrumbs
2 tablespoons sesame seeds
1 tablespoon finely chopped parsley
1 tablespoon mixed fresh herbs chopped, such
as chives, sage, thyme, rosemary, or
1½ teaspoons dried herbs
15 ml (1 tbsp) vegetable oil
25 g (1 oz) butter

Place the turkey fillets or chicken breasts between sheets of plastic wrap and flatten them with the smooth side of a mallet until very thin. Mix together the ingredients for the marinade and marinate the meat for at least 30 minutes. Remove from the marinade, season the flour with salt and freshly ground black pepper. Lightly beat the egg with the milk.

Mix together the breadcrumbs, sesame seeds, parsley and herbs. Toss each turkey fillet in the seasoned flour, shake off the excess, dip into the egg mixture and roll in the breadcumb mixture. Sauté in a mixture of vegetable oil and butter for about 5 minutes turning halfway through until lightly golden. These taste good with a little fresh lemon juice squeezed over them, so serve with half a lemon if you like.

Nasi Goreng

This is a delicious Indonesian recipe flavoured with peanuts and a mild curry sauce.

Makes 6 portions

2 chicken breasts cut into chunks
45 ml (3 tbsp) soy sauce
15 ml (1 tbsp) sesame oil
1 large onion, finely chopped
2 teaspoons mild curry powder
½ teaspoon turmeric
350g/12 oz long grain rice
900ml (1½ pints) chicken stock (see Chicken Soup on page 47)

30 ml (2 tbsp) vegetable oil
3 spring onions, finely sliced
1 red pepper, cored, de-seeded and finely chopped
90g (3½ oz) baby sweetcorn, cut into pieces
100 g (4 oz) frozen peas
1 tablespoon molasses or dark brown sugar
50 g (2 oz) roasted peanuts, finely chopped

Marinate the chicken in the soy sauce for at least 1 hour. Then remove the chicken and set the soy sauce marinade to one side. In a large saucepan, heat the sesame oil, add the onion, curry powder and turmeric and sauté for 4 minutes. Add the rice and cook for 1 minute, stirring to make sure that all the grains are coated. Pour in the stock and simmer for about 20 minutes or until the rice is tender.

Meanwhile, in a wok or frying pan, fry the chicken in the vegetable oil for about 3 minutes or until sealed. Add the spring onions, red pepper and baby sweetcorn and pour over the soy sauce from the marinade. Cook the vegetables for 2 to 3 minutes. Add the frozen peas and continue to cook for about 4 minutes. Then add the rice and stir in the molasses or dark brown sugar and, finally, the chopped peanuts. Simmer for a few minutes to heat through.

Teddy Bear Chicken Rissoles

The apple brings out a succulent flavour in these chicken rissoles. Shaping them into teddy bear faces is easy and quick and will add oodles of child appeal. (*See photograph opposite*)

Makes 6 teddy bears

4 chicken breasts
1 leek, very finely chopped (100 g / 4 oz)
1 apple, cored but not peeled and diced
3 or 4 fresh sage leaves, chopped, or 1 teaspoon dried sage
1 x 15 g (½ oz) chicken stock cube, finely crumbled

½ lightly beaten egg
50 g (2 oz) fresh white breadcrumbs
45 ml (3 tbsp) vegetable oil

Decoration
carrot, peas, olives, red pepper, apple

Chop the chicken breasts in a food processor for a few seconds. Transfer the chicken into a mixing bowl and stir in the remaining ingredients, apart from the vegetable oil. Form into 6 teddy bear shapes about 2 cm (¾ in) thick and 9 cm (3½ in) across. Sauté in the vegetable oil for 12 to 15 minutes, turning halfway through, or until golden and cooked through. Decorate with eyes, nose and a mouth.

Easy Yakitori Chicken

In Japan, yakitori bars are popular places to meet, eat and socialise. For extra flavour you can marinate the chicken in the sauce before cooking. You can also add other vegetables like peppers or mushrooms to the skewers if you wish.

Makes 4 skewers

45 ml (3 tbsp) sake or sherry
45 ml (3 tbsp) soy sauce
45 ml (3 tbsp) mirin
1 tablespoon sugar
2 chicken breasts or 8 boned chicken thighs
2 large spring onions or 1 leek, cut into 2.5-cm (1-inch) lengths
15 ml (1 tbsp) vegetable oil

MENU PLANNING
For a truly healthy meal, serve with a vegetable dish and follow with fruit. See Summer and Autumn Planners, pages 12 and 14.

Soak 4 bamboo skewers in water. Put the sake or sherry, soy sauce, mirin and sugar into a small saucepan, bring to the boil and simmer for 6-8 minutes or until syrupy. Cut the chicken breasts into chunks and thread on to the skewers alternately with the spring onion or leek. Stir the vegetable oil into the sauce and brush the chicken liberally with the sauce. Cook under a grill, turning and basting frequently for 10 to 12 minutes or until the chicken is cooked through.

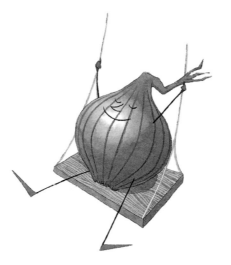

Meat

Mini Meatballs with Tomato Sauce

These meatballs are also delicious made with minced lamb and are good served with noodles or rice. The iron in red meat provides the best source of iron for you and your child as it is in a form that is absorbed well by the body. It's useful to keep a stock of these meatballs in the freezer.

Makes 4 portions

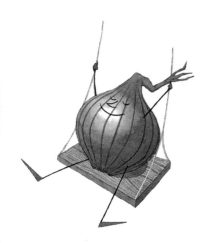

450 g (1 lb) lean minced beef
1 onion, finely chopped
1 apple, peeled and grated
50 g (2 oz) fresh white breadcrumbs
1 tablespoon chopped fresh parsley
1 chicken stock cube, finely crumbled
30 ml (2 tbsp) cold water
salt and freshly ground black pepper
30 ml (2 tbsp) vegetable oil for frying

Tomato and diced vegetable sauce
30 ml (2 tbsp) vegetable oil
175 g (6 oz) carrots, diced
50 g (2 oz) courgettes, diced
175 g (6 oz) red pepper, diced
1 onion, chopped
4 fresh ripe tomatoes, skinned, de-seeded and chopped

1 x 400 g (14 oz) can of chopped tomatoes, drained
15 ml (1 tbsp) soy sauce
30 ml (2 tbsp) tomato sauce
1½ chicken stock cubes dissolved in 900 ml (1½ pints) boiling water
a pinch of brown sugar
salt and freshly ground black pepper

> **MENU PLANNING**
> *Great at any time of day, either on its own or served with a vegetable dish.*
> *See Summer and Autumn Planners, pages 12 and 14.*

Mix together all the ingredients for the meatballs apart from the vegetable oil and chop for a few seconds in a food processor. Using your hands, form into about 20 meatballs. Heat the oil in a frying pan and sauté the meatballs for about 10 minutes until browned and sealed.

To prepare the sauce, heat 15 ml (1 tbsp) of the vegetable oil in a frying pan, add the diced carrots and sauté for 2 minutes. Add the courgette and red pepper and sauté for 4 minutes then set aside. Heat the remaining oil in the pan, sauté the onion for 2 minutes, add the fresh tomatoes, can of chopped tomatoes and continue to cook for 4 minutes.

Stir in the soy sauce, tomato sauce, chicken stock and sugar and season with salt and freshly ground black pepper. Cook for 1 minute. Add the diced vegetables, cook for 2 minutes, then add the meatballs. Transfer to a casserole and cook in an oven pre-heated to 180°C/350°F/Gas 4 for 30 minutes.

Mini Burgers with Cheese Stars

The apple in these burgers gives them a deliciously sweet taste and keeps them lovely and moist, too. Serve the burgers without the bun if you prefer.

Makes 12 burgers

450 g (1 lb) minced beef or lamb
1 onion, finely chopped (about 75 g/3 oz)
1 chicken stock cube dissolved in 30 ml (2 tbsp) hot water
1 large apple, peeled and grated (squeeze out excess juice)
1 tablespoon chopped fresh parsley

salt and freshly ground black pepper
vegetable oil for shallow frying

assorted mini rolls
lettuce
cheese slices, cut into stars
tomato relish or sauce

Mix together all the ingredients for the burgers apart from the vegetable oil and form into about 12 small burgers. Shallow fry, grill or barbecue the burgers. Cut the mini rolls in half and place the burgers on some lettuce and top with a cheese star. Leave out the cheese if your prefer and add some tomato sauce.

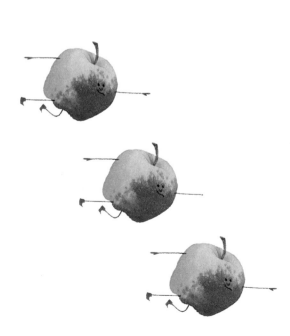

The Mini Burgers are shown overleaf

Honeyed Lamb Cutlets

Children like eating food with their fingers, which is one reason why lamb cutlets are popular. They are especially delicious if marinated in honey and soy sauce first.

Makes 6 lamb cutlets

6 lamb cutlets

Marinade
30 ml (2 tbsp) soy sauce
15 ml (1 tbsp) honey
2.5ml (½ tsp) sesame oil

Combine the ingredients for the marinade and marinate the cutlets for at least 2 hours or overnight. Cook under a pre-heated grill for about 8 minutes, turning halfway through. Brush with the marinade during cooking.

Chinese-style Mince with Noodles

I find that children love the type of food that is served in Chinese restaurants and are particularly partial to noodle dishes. Here's one that's made with lots of fresh vegetables and minced meat and my panel of tasters thought it was 'yummy'.

Makes 4 portions

100 g (4 oz) medium egg noodles
45 ml (3 tbsp) vegetable oil
1 large onion, cut into strips
350 g (12 oz) minced meat
1 clove garlic, crushed
100 g (4 oz) carrots, cut into matchsticks
50 g (2 oz) baby corn, cut lengthways and then cut in half again
100 g (4 oz) courgettes, cut into matchsticks
100 g (4 oz) beansprouts

100 g (4 oz) button mushrooms, sliced
50 g (2 oz) red pepper, cut into strips
salt and freshly ground black pepper

Sauce
1 chicken stock cube dissolved in 300 ml (½ pint) boiling water
30 ml (2 tbsp) oyster sauce
30 ml (2 tbsp) sake or sherry

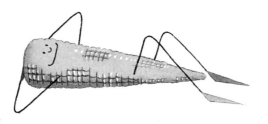
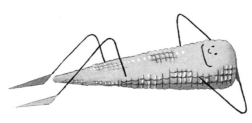

Cook the egg noodles in boiling water according to the packet instructions and set aside. Heat 15 ml (1 tbsp) of the oil in a wok or frying pan and sauté one-third of the onion for 3 minutes. Add the minced meat and stir-fry for about 6 minutes, then set aside.

Put the remaining oil in the pan and sauté the rest of the onion and the garlic for about 3 minutes. Add the carrot and baby corn and cook for 4 minutes, then add the courgette, beansprouts, mushrooms and red pepper and continue to stir-fry for 6 minutes. Return the cooked minced meat to the pan together with the cooked noodles and stir-fry for 2 minutes. Combine the ingredients for the sauce and add this to the pan, stirring for 2 minutes. Season to taste.

Lloyd's Leg of Lamb

This is absolutely delicious on a barbecue in summer but also works well in the oven. The lamb is also good eaten cold the next day. Ask your butcher to butterfly a leg of lamb for you – you will end up with a boned, flattened cut of lamb that is easy to carve and takes much less time to cook. This can be served with couscous mixed with some diced roasted vegetables like aubergine, courgette, onion and sweet pepper.

Makes 6 portions

leg of lamb, boned and butterflied

Marinade
150 ml (¼ pint) oil
30 ml (2 tbsp) walnut oil
150 ml (¼ pint) red wine
1 teaspoon oregano
60 ml (4 tbsp) lemon juice
2 or 3 garlic cloves, crushed
2 tablespoons chopped parsley

1 teaspoon sea salt
¼ teaspoon ground black pepper

> **MENU PLANNING**
> *A perfect dish for Sunday lunch – don't forget the crumble.*
> *See Winter Planner, page 16.*

Mix all the ingredients for the marinade together. Trim away as much excess fat from the lamb as you can. Pierce the lamb all over with the sharp point of a knife and place in a large polythene bag together with the marinade. Tie up the bag and leave in the fridge for 12 to 24 hours, turning frequently until ready to cook.

Barbecue over indirect heat until cooked through. Alternatively, pre-heat the oven to 220°C/425°F/Gas 7. Place the lamb on a rack over a roasting tin and roast in the oven for between 40 minutes and 1 hour depending on its weight and how you like it cooked. Take the lamb out of the oven and let it rest under foil for 15 to 20 minutes before carving across the grain into slices.

Marinated Beef with Vegetables

This delicious quick and easy to prepare beef stir-fry is bound to become a family favourite. It makes a great all-in-one meal.

Makes 4 to 5 portions

225 g (8 oz) beef fillet, rump or sirloin cut into strips

Marinade
15 ml (1 tbsp) soy sauce
15 ml (1 tbsp) sake or sherry
5 ml (1 tsp) sesame oil
1 teaspoon cornflour

175 g (6 oz) pasta twirls
45 ml (3 tbsp) sunflower oil
1 clove garlic, crushed
1 onion, thinly sliced
100 g (4 oz) carrots, sliced or cut into stars

175 g (6 oz) new potatoes
100 g (4 oz) French beans, topped and tailed
100 g (4 oz) red pepper, cut into strips
salt and freshly ground black pepper

Sauce
½ chicken stock cube dissolved in 90 ml (6 tbsp) boiling water
2.5 ml (½ tsp) rice wine vinegar
5 ml (1 tsp) soy sauce
1 teaspoon sugar
½ teaspoon cornflour

TIP
You can marinade foods in plastic bags instead of bowls that you have to wash up. Be sure you flip the bag from time to time to make sure everything gets a good soak.

Mix together the ingredients for the marinade and marinate the beef strips for at least 20 minutes. Cook the pasta in a large pan of lightly salted boiling water according to the instructions on the packet, drain, set aside and keep warm. Steam the carrots, potatoes and French beans for about 6 minutes or until tender.

Meanwhile, heat 15 ml (1 tbsp) of the vegetable oil in a wok or frying pan and stir-fry the beef for 3 minutes. Take out the beef and set aside. In the same pan, heat the remaining oil and sauté the garlic and onion for 3 minutes. Mix together all the ingredients for the sauce. Add the red pepper to the onion and cook for 2 minutes, cut the potatoes into slices and add these together with the carrots, French beans and beef and season with some salt and freshly ground black pepper. Stir in the sauce and cooked pasta and cook for 2 minutes.

Marinated Beef Skewers

Marinating cubes of beef in this sauce gives them a delicious flavour and also tenderises the meat. This is a particular favourite of my three children. If you prefer, you can make these skewers very successfully without the vegetables.

Makes 3 to 4 portions

12 oz fillet steak cut into cubes

Marinade
12 mm (½ in) ginger root, grated
1 clove garlic, crushed
15 ml (1 tbsp) dark soy sauce
5 ml (1 tsp) rice wine vinegar
15 ml (1 tbsp) vegetable oil
15 ml (1 tbsp) honey

½ red pepper, cut into chunks
1 small onion, cut into chunks
4 button mushrooms
vegetable oil

MENU PLANNING
*Grill on the barbecue and serve with salad.
See Summer Planner, page 12.*

Mix together all the ingredients for the marinade and marinate the cubes of beef for at least 1 hour. Toss the red pepper, onion and mushrooms in a little vegetable oil and thread on to the skewers alternately with the cubes of beef. Place on aluminium foil in a grill pan and grill for 3 to 4 minutes each side under a medium grill.

Maria's Luscious Lamb

Maria is a fabulous Portuguese cook and this is one of her specialities. This cut of lamb cooked on the bone is full of flavour and is very tender. For children it's best to remove the lamb from the bone, but for adults one small-sized shank each is ideal.

Makes 2 portions

2 shanks of lamb
2 shallots, chopped
1 teaspoon ground cumin
½ teaspoon turmeric
1 teaspoon paprika
½ teaspoon cayenne pepper

salt
30 ml (2 tbsp) olive oil
½ glass white wine (optional)
200 ml (6½ fl oz) stock (lamb, chicken or vegetable) (see Chicken Soup on page 47)
1 bay leaf

Sprinkle the shallots and spices over the lamb, season with a little salt and pour over the olive oil. Leave to marinate for a few hours. Pre-heat the oven to 160°C/325°F/Gas 3. Brown the lamb well in a large casserole on a stove or cook in a hot oven in a roasting tin until browned. Add the wine, stock and bay leaf. Cover the casserole or cover the roasting tin with foil and cook in the oven for 1½ hours for small shanks or 2 hours for larger, until tender.

Peter's Jamaican Patties

A friend of mine leads a rather exotic life constantly travelling around the world. This is a speciality at his home in Jamaica, where many famous guests, including Prince Edward, Drew Barrymore, Winston Churchill and Noel Coward have enjoyed eating them. Any extra patties can be frozen uncooked. Simply defrost, brush with melted butter and then cook in the oven following the instructions below.

Makes about 20 patties

1 large onion, finely chopped
1 clove garlic, crushed
½ small red pepper, cored, de-seeded and diced
30 ml (2 tbsp) vegetable oil
350 g (12 oz) lean minced beef
3 ripe tomatoes, skinned, de-seeded and chopped
30 ml (2 tbsp) tomato sauce
1 tablespoon mild curry powder

½ teaspoon fresh thyme or 1 tablespoon fresh chopped parsley
15 ml (1 tbsp) powdered chicken stock dissolved in 15 ml (1 tbsp) boiling water
salt and freshly ground black pepper

1 x 400 g (14 oz) pack fresh filo pastry or buy frozen and allow it to defrost
75 g (3 oz) butter, melted

Heat the oil in a large frying pan. Sauté the onion, garlic and red pepper for 4 to 5 minutes. Add the mince and brown thoroughly, using a fork to break down any lumps. Add the rest of the ingredients for the filling to the pan and cook over a medium high heat for about 10 minutes, stirring occasionally.

Pre-heat the oven to 180°C/350°F/Gas 4. Lay the filo pastry out flat (I use pre-cut 30 x 18 cm/12 x 7 in strips) and cover with a damp tea-towel. Place one sheet of pastry on the work surface and brush with the melted butter. Fold the pastry in half lengthways and brush again with butter.

Place 1 tablespoon of the meat filling on one edge of the strip leaving a border on the edge. Fold over the corner to make a triangle, then keep folding the parcel over on itself, along the length of the pastry. Seal the flap left at the end with melted butter. Repeat with the remaining pastry until all the meat filling has been used. Place the patties on a lightly greased baking sheet and brush with some more of the butter. Bake in the oven for about 20 minutes until golden and crispy.

Simon's Multi-layered Shepherd's Pie

Luckily, my husband Simon loves nursery food. His all-time favourite meal would probably be shepherd's pie followed by jelly. So, especially for him, I have concocted this rather luxurious version of a perennial family favourite. For adults you can increase the amount of Worcestershire sauce to give this a more tangy flavour.

Makes 5 portions

1 large onion, finely chopped
15 ml (1 tbsp) vegetable oil
450 g (1 lb) minced beef or lamb
1 x 400 g (14 oz) can of chopped tomatoes
300 ml (½ pint) chicken or beef stock (see Chicken Soup on page 47)
1 teaspoon mixed herbs
10 ml (2 tsp) Worcestershire sauce
15 ml (1 tbsp) tomato sauce
salt and freshly ground black pepper

450 g (1 lb) carrots, peeled and sliced
a knob of butter

550 g (1lb 4 oz) potatoes, peeled and chopped

50 g (2 oz) butter
75 ml (5 tbsp) milk

1 onion
7.5 ml (½ tbsp) vegetable oil
200 g (7 oz) frozen peas
200 ml (7 fl oz) chicken stock (see Chicken Soup on page 47)

MENU PLANNING
Warming and filling, this is a main course in its own right.
See Winter Planner, page 16.

Pre-heat the oven to 180°C/350°F/Gas 4. Heat the oil in a frying pan and sauté the onion until softened. Stir in the meat and cook until well browned, stirring occasionally. Add the tomatoes, stock, herbs, Worcestershire sauce, tomato sauce and seasoning. Bring to the boil, then reduce the heat and cover and simmer for 30 minutes.

Meanwhile cook the carrots until quite soft, then mash with the knob of butter until smooth. At the same time, cook the potatoes in boiling salted water until tender. Drain and mash them with 25 g (1 oz) of the butter, the milk and seasoning. Sauté the onion in the vegetable oil until softened, stir in the peas and pour the stock over the top. Bring to the boil and then simmer for 3 minutes.

Place the meat in the base of a glass oven-proof dish (approximately 18 cm/7 in diameter and 7.5 cm/3 in deep), top with the peas, then cover with the carrots and finally with a layer of mashed potato. Dot the top with the remaining butter and cook in the oven for about 20 minutes. Finish off for a few minutes under a pre-heated grill to brown the topping.

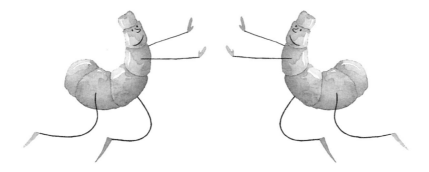

Fish

Very Easy Florentine Fillets

Fillets of tender white fish on a bed of fresh spinach covered with cheese sauce is a classic and favourite combination.

Makes 2 portions

8 oz (225 g) fresh spinach or 100 g (4 oz) frozen spinach
25 g (1 oz) butter
125 ml (4 fl oz) double cream
25 g (1 oz) Parmesan cheese, grated

225 g (8 oz) fillet of cod or haddock, filleted and skinned
15 ml (1 tbsp) milk
salt and freshly ground black pepper
20 g (¾ oz) Gruyère or Cheddar cheese, grated

Wash the spinach and remove any tough stalks. Cook in a saucepan with just a little water clinging to the leaves until wilted. Squeeze out any excess moisture. Melt half the butter and sauté the spinach for 1 minute and season to taste. (Alternatively, the spinach can be cooked in a microwave.)

Meanwhile, put the double cream, remaining butter and Parmesan cheese in a small saucepan and heat gently until the butter has melted. Lightly season the fish, put into a suitable container, dot with butter and pour over the milk. Cook in a microwave on high for about 4 minutes or until the fish flakes easily with a fork. (Alternatively, the fish can be cooked under the grill.)

Pour the cooking liquid from the fish into the cheese sauce. Arrange the spinach on a greased oven-proof dish and place the fish fillets on top. Pour over the cheese sauce and sprinkle with the grated Gruyère or Cheddar cheese. Brown under a pre-heated grill for 2 to 3 minutes.

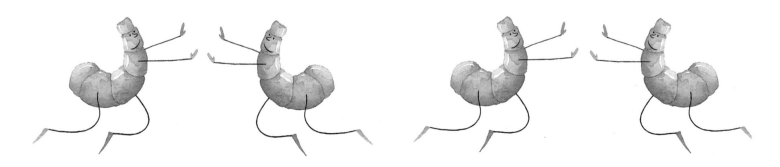

Tasty 10-minute Prawn Stir-fry

Here is a tasty stir-fry with colourful crunchy vegetables and carrot curls which is very quick to prepare. It is good served with Chinese Fried Rice (see page 132).

Makes 4 portions

100 g (4 oz) baby sweetcorn
100 g (4 oz) carrots
22.5 ml (1½ tbsp) vegetable oil
2 spring onions
100 g (4 oz) sugar snap peas or mangetout

250 ml (8 fl oz) chicken stock (see Chicken Soup on page 47)
15 ml (1 tbsp) soy sauce
30 ml (2 tbsp) sake or sherry
2 tablespoons cornflour
225 g (8 oz) cooked king prawns

Halve the sweetcorn lengthways, then cut across in half again. Using a potato peeler, cut thin strips from the carrot and cut these in half again to make long, thin, curly strips of carrot. Heat the oil in a wok or frying pan and sauté the spring onion for 1 minute. Add the other vegetables and stir-fry for 2 to 3 minutes. Remove the vegetables and set aside. Mix together the chicken stock, soy sauce, sake or sherry and cornflour. Pour the mixture into the wok and stir constantly while bringing to the boil. Reduce the heat and simmer, stirring, for 1 to 2 minutes until thickened. Stir in the prawns and the vegetables and heat through.

Teriyaki Glazed Mackerel Fillets

I think that mackerel is a very underrated fish as it has a delicious flavour, particularly when it is prepared with this teriyaki glaze. Mackerel is also very good for you as it is rich in omega-3 and the fatty acids that help to maintain a healthy heart. You could also use trout fillets to make this recipe.

Makes 2 portions

4 mackerel fillets

Marinade
30 ml (2 tbsp) soy sauce
30 ml (2 tbsp) sake or sherry
30 ml (2 tbsp) mirin

MENU PLANNING
Serve on its own or with stir-fried mushrooms and beansprouts.
See Autumn Planner, page 14.

Mix together all the ingredients for the marinade in a small saucepan and bring to the boil. Simmer for 2 to 3 minutes. Arrange the mackerel fillets in a shallow dish and pour over the hot marinade. Set aside for about 15 minutes. Heat the grill and lay the fillets on a grill pan and cook for 5 to 6 minutes on the fleshy side, brushing occasionally with the teriyaki marinade until cooked.

King Prawn Stir-fry with Sugar Snap Peas

Stir-fries make popular, quick and easy meals for the whole family, especially if you have a quantity of chicken stock ready prepared and in the freezer. This particular recipe could also be made with fresh uncooked prawns.

Makes 4 portions

300 g (10 oz) cooked king prawns (de-veined)

100 g (4 oz) button mushrooms, cut in half
150 g (5 oz) sugar snap peas

Marinade
1 egg white, lightly beaten
1 teaspoon cornflour
a pinch of salt
a pinch of ground white pepper

45 ml (3 tbsp) vegetable oil
2 eggs, lightly beaten
1 clove garlic, crushed
1 onion, thinly sliced
100 g (4 oz) baby corn, cut in half

Sauce
375 ml (12 fl oz) chicken stock (see Chicken Soup on page 47)
15 ml (1 tbsp) soy sauce
15 ml (1 tbsp) sesame oil
1½ tablespoons caster sugar
7.5 ml (½ tbsp) cider vinegar
1½ tablespoons cornflour
2 spring onions, finely sliced
a little ground white pepper

Mix together the beaten egg white, cornflour and seasoning and marinate the prawns in this mixture for about 10 minutes. To make the sauce, mix together the stock, soy sauce, sesame oil, sugar and vinegar. In a small bowl mix 45 ml (3 tbsp) of the sauce with the cornflour until smooth and then stir this into the rest of the sauce. Pour the sauce into a saucepan, bring to the boil and then simmer, stirring, for 2 to 3 minutes until thickened. Stir in the spring onions and season with the white pepper.

Strain the marinade from the prawns and discard. Heat 15 ml (1 tbsp) of the oil in a frying pan and sauté the prawns for about 2 minutes then set aside. Heat another tablespoon of oil in the pan and swirl the beaten egg around to form a thin layer and cook until set. Remove from the pan and fold it over three times like a swiss roll, cut into strips and set aside.

Add the remaining oil to the pan and sauté the garlic and onion for 2 minutes. Stir-fry the corn, button mushrooms and sugar snap peas for 6 minutes. Add the prawns and the sauce and cook for 2 minutes or until heated through.

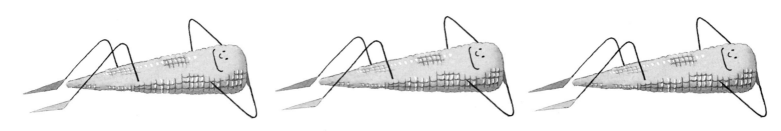

Yummy Fish in Orange Sauce

This is a great way to cook up a fillet of fresh fish in just a few minutes. As it is so easy, I make it for my own lunch sometimes. For more people, simply increase the quantities.

Makes 1 portion

1 x 225g (8 oz) fillet of cod, haddock or hake, skinned
plain flour
salt and freshly ground black pepper
20 g (¾ oz) butter
5 ml (1 tsp) soy sauce
5 ml (1 tsp) freshly squeezed orange juice

> **MENU PLANNING**
> *Equally quick to make for one person as it is for several – serve with salad and fruit. See Summer Planner, page 12.*

Season some flour with a little salt and freshly ground black pepper and coat the fish in the seasoned flour. Melt the butter in a frying pan and sauté the fish for about 5 minutes, turning occasionally. Mix together the soy sauce and orange juice, pour over the fish, turn up the heat and cook for about 1 minute.

Mermaid Morsels

These miniature fish balls are very tasty. You can use any combination of white fish available, such as cod, haddock, whiting, hake or halibut. A fishmonger should be able to prepare it for you. They are good served hot or cold.

Makes 20 balls

450 g (1 lb) minced or finely chopped mixed white fish
1 large onion, finely chopped
15 ml (1 tbsp) vegetable oil and a knob of butter plus extra for frying the fish balls
1 carrot, finely grated
1 tablespoon finely chopped fresh parsley

1 egg, lightly beaten
2 dessertspoons sugar
1 teaspoon salt
a little freshly ground black pepper
22.5 ml (1½ tbsp) cold water
2 tablespoons flour plus extra for coating the fish balls

Fry the onion in a mixture of oil and butter until soft and lightly golden. Combine the minced fish, fried onion, carrot and parsley. Beat the egg together with the sugar, salt and pepper until frothy and add the egg mixture to the minced fish. Finally, mix in the cold water and 2 tablespoons of the flour. Using your hands, form into small walnut-sized balls, roll in flour and fry in a mixture of vegetable oil and butter until golden, turning occasionally.

Spaghetti Marinara

It's very important that you only buy very fresh seafood, so always buy it from a reputable source. This is a delicious pasta sauce and you can make it quite spicy for adults by adding more chilli if you like. I would not recommend giving seafood to very young children.

Makes 4 portions

900 g (2 lb) mussels
8 large raw prawns
350 g (12 oz) spaghetti

Sauce
30 ml (2 tbsp) olive oil
4 shallots, finely chopped

1 clove garlic, crushed
2 tablespoons chopped fresh parsley
6 tablespoons dry white wine
800 g (1 lb 12 oz) can of chopped tomatoes
1 or 2 dried red chillies, crushed, or a good pinch of red pepper flakes
salt and freshly ground black pepper

Discard any mussels that are not closed, then scrub well under cold water and pull off and discard the beards. Set the mussels aside. Peel, de-vein and cut the prawns in half lengthways. Cook the spaghetti in a large pan of lightly salted water according to the instructions on the packet.

Heat the olive oil in a frying pan and sauté the shallots and garlic for 2 minutes, add the parsley and sauté for 1 minute. Add the wine, simmer for 2 minutes, then add the tomatoes and chilli(es) and simmer for 4 minutes. Add the mussels and cook for 4 to 5 minutes. Discard any mussels that do not open. Add the prawns, simmer for about 2 minutes and season to taste.

Drain the spaghetti, return to the warm pan, add the marinara sauce and toss gently. If you like, remove the mussels from their shells (discard any where the shells have not opened) and mix with the spaghetti.

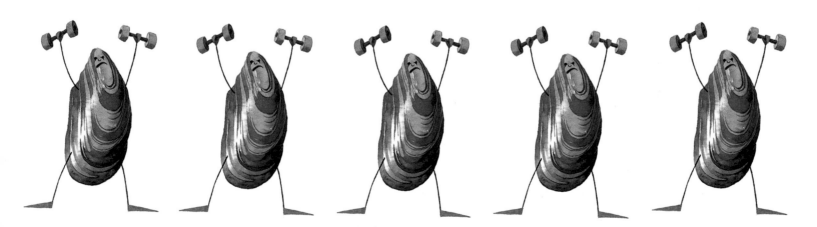

Simply Super Salmon Teriyaki

My husband Simon and I both love Japanese food and this is one of my favourite fish recipes. It's a great favourite with my children too and it's well worth investing in a bottle of sake or sherry and mirin (a sweet Japanese cooking wine) as you will want to make this recipe over and over again. Serve with basmati rice.

Makes 4 portions

4 x 150 g (5 oz) thick fillets of salmon, skinned

30 ml (2 tbsp) vegetable oil
150 g (5 oz) button mushrooms, sliced
150 g (5 oz) beansprouts

Marinade
40ml (1½ fl oz) soy sauce
50 ml (2 fl oz) sake or sherry
25 ml (1 fl oz) mirin
1 tablespoon sugar

> **MENU PLANNING**
> *For a smart dinner, serve with basmati rice and follow with a fruit brulée.*
> *See Summer Planner, page 12.*

Mix the ingredients for the marinade together in a saucepan and stir over a medium heat until the sugar has dissolved. Marinate the salmon in the sauce for 10 minutes.

Heat half the oil and sauté the mushrooms for 2 minutes, then add the beansprouts and cook for 2 minutes more. Meanwhile, drain the salmon, reserving the marinade. Heat the remaining oil in a frying pan and sauté the salmon for 1 or 2 minutes on each side or until slightly browned. Pour away the excess oil from the frying pan. Alternatively, it is particularly good if you cook the salmon on a very hot griddle pan brushed with a little oil.

Whichever method you choose, after 2 minutes pour a little of the teriyaki sauce over the salmon and continue to cook for a few minutes, basting occasionally. Simmer the remaining teriyaki sauce in a small saucepan until thickened. Divide the vegetables between four plates, place the salmon on top and pour the teriyaki sauce over the fish.

Fishing for Compliments

It's a shame that for many children the only fish that they enjoy eating is fish fingers. However, this is a very tasty fish recipe that I have invented for children although it's also delicious for the whole family and may well tempt even the most reluctant fish eater.

Makes 2 portions

Sauce
250 ml (8 fl oz) chicken stock (see Chicken Soup on page 47)
10 ml (2 tsp) soy sauce
5 ml (1 tsp) sesame oil
1 tablespoon sugar
5 ml (1 tsp) cider vinegar
1 tablespoon cornflour
1 spring onion, finely sliced

350 g (12 oz) plaice, sole or cod fillets skinned and cut into strips about 6.5 cm (2½ in) long
15 ml (1 tbsp) lemon juice
15 ml (1 tbsp) water
1 tablespoon chopped onion
45 ml (3 tbsp) vegetable oil
100 g (4 oz) courgettes, cut into strips
50 g (2 oz) red pepper, cut into strips
plain flour
salt and freshly ground black pepper

Rinse the fish fillets and pat dry with paper towels. Mix together the lemon juice, water and chopped onion and marinate the fish in this mixture for about 30 minutes.

To make the sauce, mix together the stock, soy sauce, sesame oil, sugar, vinegar and cornflour. Pour the sauce into a saucepan, bring to the boil and then simmer, stirring, for 2 to 3 minutes until thickened and smooth. Stir in the spring onion.

Heat 15 ml (1 tbsp) of the vegetable oil in a pan and sauté the courgette and red pepper for 4 minutes. Strain the marinade from the fish and discard (including the onion), coat the fish lightly in seasoned flour. Heat the remaining oil in a pan and sauté the fish for about 3 minutes each side or until cooked. Add the vegetables, pour over the sauce and cook for 2 minutes.

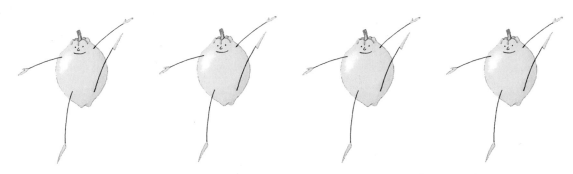

Salmon Fillets in a Watercress Sauce

Salmon has become much more plentiful and cheaper in recent years. This combination of salmon in a creamy watercress sauce works well and it is good served with mangetout and new potatoes.

Serves 4

450 g (1 lb) salmon fillets, skinned
salt and freshly ground black pepper
25 g (1 oz) melted butter
a good squeeze of lemon juice
50 g (2 oz) finely chopped shallots
25 g (1 oz) butter

175 g (6 oz) courgettes, sliced
150 g (¼ pint) chicken stock or fish stock (see
Chicken Soup on page 47)
50 g (2 oz) watercress, leaves only
45–60 ml (3–4 tbsp) double cream

Pre-heat the oven to 180°C/350°F/Gas 4. Lightly season the salmon, brush with melted butter and squeeze over the lemon juice. Cook on High in a microwave for about 6 minutes or until the fish flakes easily with a fork. If you do not have a microwave, place each fillet on a piece of foil, lightly season, brush with melted butter, add a squeeze of lemon and wrap the foil so that there is room around the fish but the parcel is sealed. Bake in the oven for 20 to 25 minutes or until the fish is cooked.

Meanwhile, sauté the shallots in the butter for 2 minutes, add the courgettes and sauté for 2 to 3 minutes. Pour the chicken stock over the courgettes, bring to the boil, reduce the heat and cook for about 5 minutes. Add the watercress and continue to cook for 2 minutes. Remove from the heat. Purée in a blender, stir in the cream, season to taste and pour the sauce over the salmon fillets. Heat through before serving.

Posh Fish Fingers

Crushed cornflakes make a delicious coating for fried fish. Serve with oven-baked chips and maybe wrap them up in a newspaper or a comic for fun. My children like fish and chips sprinkled with a little malt vinegar.

*Makes 4
portions*

450 g (1 lb) cod, haddock, plaice or hake
fillets, skinned
salt and freshly ground black pepper
50 g (2 oz) plain flour

1 egg, lightly beaten
50 g (2 oz) cornflakes
1 tablespoon fresh chopped parsley
vegetable oil for frying

Put the fish into four portions and season. Coat in flour and then dip into the beaten egg. Crush the cornflakes (this can be done by putting them in a bag and crushing them with a rolling pin) and mix with the chopped parsley. Roll the fish fillets into the cornflake mixture to coat and fry in vegetable oil until golden and cooked through.

Perfect Paella

This paella is simple and quick to prepare. It is very important that you use only fresh live mussels and any uncooked mussels that are already open should be discarded. Once the mussels are cooked the shells should open, but do not eat cooked mussels if the shells remain closed. You can sometimes buy bags of frozen or fresh mixed seafood, which could also be used for this recipe and then you may find that the mussels are already cooked and out of their shells.

Makes 4 portions

1 clove garlic, crushed
1 onion, chopped
15 ml (1 tbsp) olive oil
1 red pepper, cut into strips
300 g (10 oz) easy cook rice
1 teaspoon turmeric
1 teaspoon mild chilli powder
1.2 litres (2 pints) chicken stock (see Chicken Soup on page 47)
1 bay leaf
2 tablespoons chopped fresh parsley

150 g (5 oz) fresh prawns
225 g (8 oz) fresh clams
350 g (12 oz) mussels
100 g (4 oz) frozen peas

MENU PLANNING

On a hot summer's night, eat this outside and follow with a fruit brulée. See Summer Planner, page 12.

Sauté the onion and garlic in the oil for 1 minute. Add the red pepper and cook for another 3 minutes. Add the rice and the turmeric and chilli powder and stir in the pan for about 1 minute. Pour in the stock, add the bay leaf and cook for 15 minutes over a medium heat. Add the parsley and cook for about 5 minutes. Turn the heat up, add the fish and frozen peas and cook for 1 to 2 minutes over a high heat. Reduce the heat and cover and cook for about 5 minutes or until the fish is cooked. Remove any shells that haven't opened.

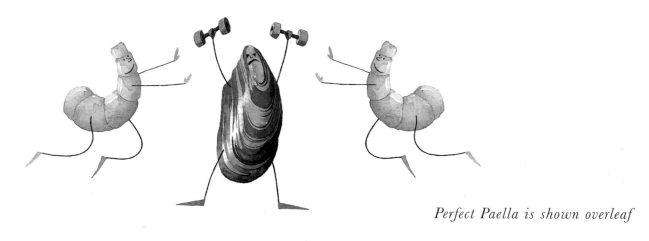

Perfect Paella is shown overleaf

Evelyn's Tasty Fish Pie

This is one of the recipes that my mother used to make and I remember how much I enjoyed eating it as a child. Now I make it for my children.

Makes 4 to 5 portions

450 g (1 lb) fillets cod or haddock, skinned
plain flour
salt and freshly ground black pepper
1 egg, beaten
100 g (4 oz) fine breadcrumbs
vegetable oil
1 onion, finely chopped
15 ml (1 tbsp) olive oil
100 g (4 oz) green pepper, cored, de-seeded and chopped
150 g (5 oz) red pepper, cored, de-seeded and chopped
1 x 400 g (14 oz) can of chopped tomatoes
30 ml (2 tbsp) tomato purée
1 tablespoon chopped fresh parsley

Cheese sauce
25 g (1 oz) butter
25 g (1 oz) plain flour
250 ml (8 fl oz) milk
75 g (3 oz) Cheddar cheese, grated
40 g (1½ oz) Parmesan cheese, grated

MENU PLANNING
For an informal lunch, follow this pie with some apricot cookies.
See Spring Planner, page 10.

Pre-heat the oven to 180°C/350°F/Gas 4. Cut the fillets of fish into about eight pieces. Dip each fillet into seasoned flour, then into the lightly beaten egg and finally coat in breadcrumbs. Sauté in the oil until golden on both sides and then drain on kitchen paper.

Sauté the onion in the olive oil for 2 to 3 minutes, add the peppers and continue to cook for 5 minutes. Drain the juice from the tomatoes and add the chopped tomatoes to the peppers together with the tomato purée. Cook for 5 minutes. Season to taste and sprinkle with the parsley. Mix the cooked fish with the tomato sauce.

To make the cheese sauce, melt the butter, stir in the flour and cook for 1 minute over a low heat to make a roux. Gradually whisk in the milk, stirring, over a medium heat until thickened. Bring to the boil and then cook for 1 minute. Remove from the heat and stir in two-thirds of the Cheddar and Parmesan cheese, reserving the remainder for sprinkling over the top of the fish pie.

Put the fish in tomato sauce into an oven-proof dish, cover with the cheese sauce and sprinkle the remaining cheese on top. Cook in the oven for 20 minutes. Brown the top under a pre-heated grill for a few minutes to finish off.

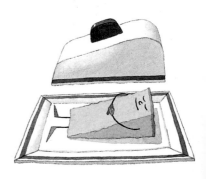

Soupa Tuna Tagliatelle

This is a tasty and nutritious pasta dish that is quick and easy to make for the whole family using store cupboard ingredients, including a can of tomato sauce.

Makes 6 portions

225 g (8 oz) green and white tagliatelle
25 g (1 oz) butter
1 small onion, finely chopped
1 heaped tablespoon cornflour
1 x 405 g (14 oz) can of cream
of tomato soup
2 tablespoons chopped fresh parsley
½ teaspoon dried mixed herbs
1 x 400 g (14 oz) can of tuna

Cheese sauce
25 g (1 oz) butter

20 g (¾ oz) flour
375 ml (12 fl oz) milk
a pinch of dried mustard powder
100 g (4 oz) Cheddar cheese, grated
1 tablespoon snipped chives
50 g (2 oz) sweetcorn, cooked
salt and freshly ground black pepper

Topping
25 g (1 oz) brown breadcrumbs
25 g (1 oz) Cheddar cheese, grated
1 tablespoon freshly grated Parmesan cheese

Pre-heat the oven to 180°C/350°F/Gas 4. Cook the tagliatelle in a large saucepan of lightly salted boiling water until just tender. Melt the butter in a saucepan and sauté the onion until softened. Mix the cornflour with 30 ml (2 tbsp) cold water until dissolved. Mix the cornflour mixture, tomato soup, parsley and herbs with the sautéed onion and cook over a medium heat for about 5 minutes or until the sauce has thickened. Stir the tuna fish into the sauce and mix with the cooked tagliatelle.

To make the cheese sauce, put the butter, flour and milk into a saucepan and cook over a medium heat. Using a balloon whisk, keep whisking the mixture until it boils and thickens to form a smooth sauce. Add the mustard powder and simmer for 2 to 3 minutes. Remove from the heat and stir in 75 g (3 oz) of the cheese until melted. Stir in the chives and cooked sweetcorn and season to taste.

Arrange the tuna and pasta mixture in a 25 x 20 cm (10 x 8 in) oven-proof dish and pour over the cheese sauce. Mix together the breadcrumbs and grated cheeses and scatter these over the top. Cook in the oven for 20 minutes. Brown under a hot grill for a few minutes before serving.

Chinese Noodles with Prawns and Beansprouts

This noodle dish is quick and easy to prepare and very versatile. You can use shredded chicken or pork instead of the prawns or perhaps strips of omelette if you are vegetarian. You can also substitute other vegetables like strips of courgette, carrot or baby sweetcorn. This makes a good accompaniment to stir-fries.

Makes 4 portions

175 g (6 oz) medium egg noodles
30 ml (2 tbsp) vegetable oil
4 spring onions, sliced
½ to 1 teaspoon finely chopped red chilli
(optional)
1 clove garlic, crushed
1 tablespoon fresh chopped parsley
100 g (4 oz) button, oyster or shitake
mushrooms sliced
100 g (4 oz) large cooked peeled prawns
45 ml (3 tbsp) oyster sauce
1 teaspoon caster sugar

125 ml (4 fl oz) water
100 g (4 oz) fresh beansprouts
125 ml (4 fl oz) chicken stock (see Chicken
Soup on page 47)

MENU PLANNING
*Vegetable soup is a good starter for this more
filling main course.
See Winter Planner, page 16.*

Drop the noodles into a large pan of boiling water. Return to the boil and simmer for 4 minutes. Drain and set aside.

Meanwhile, heat the vegetable oil in a wok or frying pan and stir-fry the spring onions, chilli (if using), garlic and parsley for 1 minute. Add the mushrooms and prawns and stir-fry for 2 minutes. Add the oyster sauce, caster sugar and water. Stir in the beansprouts and stock and cook for 2 minutes. Return the noodles to the pan and heat through.

Vegetarian Dishes

Perfect Chinese Fried Rice

This tends to be very popular with children and can be served as an accompaniment to many of the recipes in this book.

*Makes 4 to 5
portions*

200 g (7 oz) basmati rice
65 g (2½ oz) carrots, finely chopped
75 g (3 oz) frozen peas
5 ml (1 tsp) vegetable oil
2 eggs, lightly beaten
25 g (1 oz) butter
65 g (2½ oz) onion, finely chopped
30 ml (2 tbsp) soy sauce

MENU PLANNING
*Chinese fried rice is a great accompaniment
for many of the recipes in this book. See
Spring, Summer and Autumn Planners,
pages 10, 12 and 14.*

Cook the rice according to the instructions on the packet. Transfer the rice to a large bowl, add the peas and carrot and set aside to cool. Heat the vegetable oil in a pan, add the eggs and scramble over a medium heat, breaking up into little pieces. Melt the butter in a wok or large frying pan and sauté the onion for 1 minute. Add the cooled rice mixture, the scrambled egg, the soy sauce and a little ground pepper. Stir-fry the rice for about 5 minutes.

Baked Marrow with a Cheesy Topping

If your child isn't too keen on eating vegetables, try this tasty recipe. It also makes a delicious accompaniment to an adult meal – it is works especially well with poultry.

Makes 4 portions

1 medium-sized marrow
salt
1 onion, chopped
1 tablespoon parsley

30 ml (2 tbsp) vegetable oil
1 x 400 g (14 oz) can of chopped tomatoes
1 tablespoon fresh basil, torn into small pieces
100 g (4 oz) Cheddar cheese, grated

Peel and halve the marrow, scoop out the seeds and cut into 2.5 cm (1 in) cubes. Place in a colander, sprinkle with salt and leave for about 30 minutes. Rinse under the tap and pat dry.

Pre-heat the oven to 190°C/375°F/Gas 5. Sauté the onion and parsley in the oil until softened, add the tomatoes and cook for about 4 minutes. Add the marrow and basil, simmer for 10 to 15 minutes and season to taste. Transfer to an oven-proof dish, stir in 75 g (3 oz) of the cheese and sprinkle the remaining cheese on top. Bake in the oven for 30 minutes or until browned.

Denise's Easy Spinach Pie

Denise is the mother of three boys with big appetites, so she likes to make really filling food that is healthy too. Here is a family dish that she makes which is popular with everyone.

Makes 8 portions

500 g (1 lb 2 oz) fresh spinach (or use
225 g/8 oz frozen spinach)
225 g (8 oz) feta cheese, crumbled
100 g (4 oz) Cheddar cheese, grated
3 eggs

a generous pinch of ground nutmeg
freshly ground black pepper
300 g (10 oz) shortcrust pastry
330 g (10 oz) puff pastry

Pre-heat the oven to 190°C/375°F/Gas 5. Carefully wash the fresh spinach and cook in a large saucepan with some lightly salted boiling water for 3 to 4 minutes and then drain. Press out any excess water (this can be done by putting the spinach in a sieve and use a wooden spoon to press out the water) then chop the spinach for a few seconds in a food processor. Combine the cheeses, whisk two of the eggs and add to the cheeses. Mix together the chopped spinach, cheese and egg mixture and season with a little pepper and nutmeg.

Roll out the shortcrust pastry and use to line the base and sides of a greased 25 cm (10 in) quiche dish. Prick the base of the pastry and bake blind in the oven for 10 minutes. Fill with the spinach and cheese mixture. Roll out the remaining pastry and lay over the top of the quiche. Roll the pastry and tuck any excess inside the sides of the quiche dish and pinch the edges together. Brush the top of the pastry with the remaining egg, lightly beaten, and sprinkle with the sesame seeds. ake for about 20 minutes.

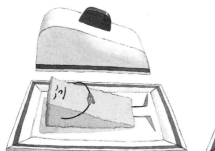
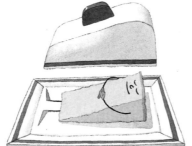

ANTIOXIDANTS

Vitamins A,C and E are known as antioxidants. They are thought to help protect against free radicals, destructive molecules that damage cells and DNA. If left unchecked, these unstable and potentially harmful chemicals can create conditions that may precipitate heart disease and cancer.

Experts now believe that a diet rich in fruits and vegetables may reduce heart disease by up to 20%. Vitamins C, E and betacarotene (the plant form of vitamin A) can help neutralize free radicals.

Summer Risotto

I like to make my risotto in a large frying pan. You will need to add the liquid to the rice little by little, waiting to add more until all the liquid has been absorbed and stirring frequently. It usually takes about 30 minutes to prepare, depending on your pan and your stove. Stir in a little extra stock if you need to re-heat the risotto.

Makes 4 portions

900 ml (1½ pints) vegetable stock or chicken stock (see Chicken Soup on page 47)
125 ml (4 fl oz) white wine or use an extra 125 ml (4 fl oz) stock
1 onion, finely chopped
1 garlic clove, crushed
15 ml (1 tbsp) olive oil
25 g (1 oz) butter
100 g (4 oz) red pepper, chopped
200 g (7 oz) arborio (risotto) rice
125 g (4½ oz) courgettes, diced

2 medium tomatoes, skinned, de-seeded and chopped (about 225 g/8 oz)
25 g (1 oz) Parmesan cheese, grated
a knob of butter
salt and freshly ground black pepper

MENU PLANNING
Follow this with a refreshing frozen yoghurt.
See Summer Planner, page 12.

Bring the stock to the boil and then allow to simmer. Add the wine if using. Heat the oil and butter in a large frying pan and sauté the onion and garlic for 1 minute. Add the chopped pepper to the onion and cook for 5 minutes. Add the rice and, making sure that it is well coated, stir for 1 minute. Add one or two ladlefuls of hot stock and simmer, stirring, until it has been absorbed, then add another ladleful of stock. Continue adding the stock a little at a time and simmer until the rice absorbs the liquid before adding more, stirring quite frequently.

After 10 minutes, add the diced courgette and tomato. When all the stock has been added and the rice is cooked (probably another 15 to 20 minutes), stir in the Parmesan cheese and the knob of butter and season to taste.

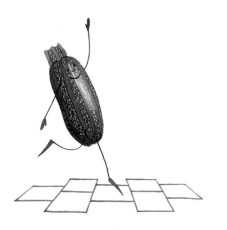

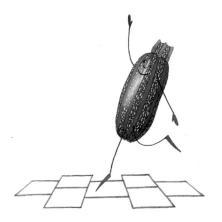

Perfect Baked Potatoes

The best potatoes to choose are floury varieties like Desirée, King Edward or Maris Piper. You can also make mini baked potatoes by using normal size potatoes, in which case the cooking time will be shorter. You could also try making baked sweet potatoes and serve these with butter and a little freshly ground black pepper.

Makes 4 portions

4 large baking potatoes
olive oil (optional)

salt and freshly ground black pepper
100 g (4 oz) cold butter

Pre-heat the oven to 200°C/400°F/Gas 6. Wash and dry the potatoes and prick the skins a few times with a fork. If you want extra crisp skins then rub the skins with a few drops of olive oil and sprinkle with a little salt before baking. Place on the centre shelf in the oven for 1 to 1½ hours (the cooking time will depend on the size of the potatoes). To check if the potatoes are cooked, squeeze gently to see if they feel soft.

Cut a cross in the top of each potato and squeeze the sides to open them up. Sprinkle with a little salt and freshly ground black pepper and top with butter. Alternatively, cut each of the potatoes in half lengthways and scoop out the flesh and mash with a little milk, butter and seasoning.

TO MICROWAVE

Prick the potatoes as usual and wrap each one in absorbent kitchen paper. Cook on High for 6 to 7 minutes for one potato or about 12 minutes for two potatoes and 18 to 20 minutes for four potatoes (timings will differ depending on the size of the potatoes).

OTHER GOOD TOPPINGS

Sour cream and chives
Plain or curried baked beans
Tuna, mayonnaise and sweetcorn
Bacon cooked until crisp and then crumbled
Vegetables such as broccoli and carrots in a cheese sauce
Smoked ham, grated Cheddar cheese, crème fraîche or chives

Fluffy Baked Potatoes

Makes 4 portions

4 baking potatoes, scrubbed and pricked
50 g (2 oz) butter
45 ml (3 tbsp) double cream or milk

2 eggs, separate
75 g (3 oz) Cheddar cheese, grated
salt and freshly ground black pepper

Pre-heat the oven to 190°C/375°F/Gas 5. Cut each potato in half, scoop out the flesh into a large saucepan leaving enough around the sides so that they still retain their shape. Add the butter, cream, egg yolks and 50 g (2 oz) of the cheese to the potato flesh. Mash together until smooth and season to taste. Whisk the egg whites until stiff and fold into the potato mixture. Carefully spoon this back into the potato skins and sprinkle with the remaining grated cheese. Bake in the oven for 15 minutes until golden. Serve immediately.

Mini Baked Potatoes

For a change, how about making mini baked potatoes using new potatoes. The potato's best source of fibre and nutrients is in the skin and in the flesh just under the skin. Potatoes are a good source of carbohydrate, which provides energy, and are also a useful and cheap source of vitamin C.

Makes 4 portions

450 g (1 lb) new potatoes
15 ml (1 tbsp) olive oil
1 teaspoon dried mixed herbs
2 teaspoons coarse sea salt

Toppings
Sour cream and chives
Hummus
Taramasalata
Tuna mayonnaise and sweetcorn
Baked beans
Cottage cheese with chives

Pre-heat the oven to 200°C/400°F/Gas 6. Scrub and dry the potatoes. Prick the skins with a fork and mix them with the olive oil and herbs, tossing them in a bowl to coat. Place the potatoes on a baking sheet and sprinkle with the sea salt. Bake for 25 to 30 minutes or until they are crisp and tender. Cut a cross in the top of each potato, squeeze them gently to open them up and fill with a topping of your choice or just simply with a knob of butter.

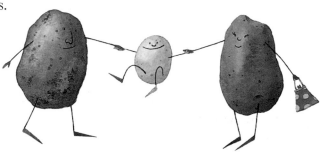

Gratin of Courgette

This has a light soufflé-type consistency and makes a delicious light lunch with a salad or can be served as a tasty accompaniment to a meal and looks elegant enough for a dinner party. (*See photograph opposite*)

Makes 6 portions

45 ml (3 tbsp) vegetable oil
500 g (1 lb 2 oz) courgettes, topped and tailed
and thinly sliced
salt and freshly ground black pepper

2 tablespoons chopped fresh parsley
4 eggs
125 ml (4 fl oz) crème fraîche
150 g (5 oz) Gruyère cheese, grated

Pre-heat the oven to 180°C/350°F/Gas 4. Heat the oil in a frying pan and season the courgettes with some salt and freshly ground black pepper. Sauté these together with the parsley over a low heat for about 20 minutes or until softened. Using a fork, beat the eggs, then beat in the crème fraîche, Gruyère cheese and a little seasoning. Stir in the courgettes and spoon the mixture into an oven-proof dish measuring approximately 25 x 20 cm (10 x 8 in) and cook in the oven for 20 to 25 minutes.

Courgette Fritters

If your children aren't keen on eating vegetables then try these – they are delicious and were very popular with my tasting panel – even the confirmed vegetable haters.

Makes 4 portions

450 g (1 lb) courgettes
salt and freshly ground black pepper
250 ml (8 fl oz) water

4 tablespoons cornflour
8 tablespoons plain flour
vegetable oil for deep frying

Wash and dry the courgettes and trim off the ends. Cut them into sticks about 6 cm (2¼ in) long and 2 cm (¾ in) wide and season them with salt and pepper. Beat together the water, cornflour, plain flour and some salt and pepper to form a thin batter.

Heat the oil in a deep fat fryer with a basket filled with oil to a depth of about 5 cm (2 in). Alternatively, you could use a heavy pan and a metal slotted spoon or strainer. Heat the oil until it reaches a temperature of 190°C/375°F (you can tell when it is hot enough for frying if a piece of vegetable sizzles as it touches the oil). Dip the courgette sticks into the batter and fry them until crispy and golden. Lift out the basket or remove the courgette fritters with a slotted spoon or strainer. Drain on absorbent paper and serve immediately.

Super Vegetarian Spring Rolls

Spring rolls are perennial favourites and these are light, crispy and delicious. The sauce is optional.

Makes 15 vegetarian spring rolls

22.5 ml (1½ tbsp) vegetable oil
1 clove garlic, crushed
1 onion, thinly sliced
175 g (6 oz) carrots, cut into thin strips
100 g (4 oz) baby corn, cut into thin strips
100 g (4 oz) button mushrooms, cut into thin strips
50 g (2 oz) red pepper, cut into thin strips
225 g (8 oz) Chinese cabbage, shredded
1 tablespoon fresh chopped parsley
15 ml (1 tbsp) oyster sauce
7.5 ml (½ tbsp) soy sauce
½ x vegetable or chicken stock cube, finely crumbled
salt and freshly ground black pepper
1 egg, lightly beaten
twelve 20 cm (8 in) square spring roll wrappers
vegetable oil for frying

Dipping sauce

150 ml (¼ pint) chicken or vegetable stock (see Chicken Soup on page 47)
7.5 ml (½ tbsp) soy sauce
1 teaspoon sugar
2.5 ml (½ tsp) cider vinegar
1 tablespoon finely sliced spring onion
½ teaspoon cornflour

> **MENU PLANNING**
> *Make these in advance and freeze before frying – then serve on their own or following a bowl of soup.*
> *See Winter Planner, page 16.*

Heat the oil in a wok or frying pan and sauté the onion and garlic for 2 minutes. Add the carrots and baby corn and stir-fry for 3 minutes. Add the mushrooms, red pepper, Chinese cabbage and parsley and stir-fry for 3 minutes. Add the oyster sauce, soy sauce and crumbled chicken or vegetable stock cube, season with a little salt and pepper and cook for 2 minutes.

Lay the spring roll wrappers diagonally on a work surface and spoon about 45 ml (3 tbsp) of the vegetable mixture about 5 cm (2 in) from the bottom of each wrapper leaving a border on either side. Roll them up, tucking in the sides to make neat parcels. Brush the flap at the end of each one with a little beaten egg to seal the spring rolls. Just before serving, deep fry a few at a time in hot oil until golden and crispy. Drain on kitchen paper.

Mix together all the ingredients for the sauce apart from the cornflour. Mix a little of the sauce with the cornflour and then pour this back into the remaining sauce and heat in a saucepan, stirring, until slightly thickened. Serve with the spring rolls.

Gratin of Carrots with a Crunchy Topping

(add crushed cornflakes once the dish has defrosted)

Carrots are an excellent source of beta-carotene, which is the plant form of vitamin A. Surprisingly, unlike most vegetables, carrots are more nutritious eaten cooked than raw. This is because the cooking process helps our bodies to absorb the vitamin A that carrots contain. Both carrots and cheese tend to be very popular with children, so this combination is a real winner. It also makes a delicious accompaniment to an adult meal.

Makes 4 portions

450 g (1 lb) carrots, sliced
1 small onion, finely chopped
50 g (2 oz) butter
37.5 ml (2½ tbsp) flour
300 ml (½ pint) semi-skimmed milk

75 g (3 oz) Gruyère cheese, grated
salt and freshly ground black pepper
1 tablespoon chopped fresh parsley
65 g (2½ oz) cornflakes

Pre-heat the oven to 180°C/350°F/Gas 4. Cook the carrots in lightly salted water until tender (about 15 minutes) and drain. Alternatively, steam or microwave the carrots until tender. Meanwhile, sauté the onion in 25 g (1 oz) butter until softened. Remove from the heat, stir in the flour and gradually pour in the milk. Return to the heat and stir until thickened and smooth. Take off the heat and stir in the cheese until melted. Season to taste.

Combine the cooked carrots and parsley with the cheese sauce and spoon into an oven-proof dish. Melt the remaining butter, crush the cornflakes and mix with the melted butter. Arrange the crushed cornflakes over the carrot gratin and cook in the oven for 15 minutes.

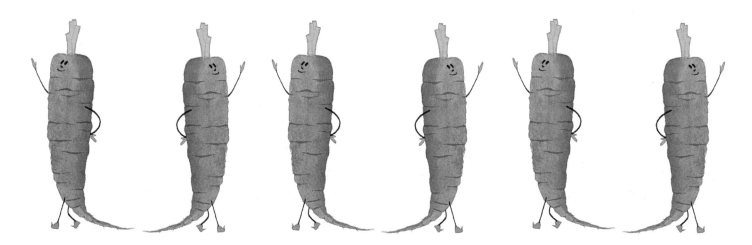

Caramelised Onion and Gruyère Tart

This is my favourite recipe for quiche and the slow cooking of the onions gives them a delicious flavour. The pastry takes only a few minutes to make in a food processor, but you could use bought shortcrust pastry instead.

Makes 8 portions

Pastry
225 g (8 oz) plain flour
a pinch of salt
½ teaspoon mustard powder
125 g (4½ oz) butter, diced
45 ml (3 tbsp) cold water

Filling
500 g (1 lb 2 oz) onions, thinly sliced
15 ml (1 tbsp) vegetable oil
15 g (½ oz) butter
salt and freshly ground black pepper
4 eggs
300 ml (½ pint) milk
300 ml (½ pint) single cream
150 g (5 oz) Gruyère cheese, grated
25 g (1 oz) Parmesan cheese, grated

> **MENU PLANNING**
> At lunch time, serve with a simple salad
> and follow with fruit.
> See Autumn Planner, page 14.

Put the flour, salt, mustard powder and butter in a food processor and process until the mixture resembles soft bread-crumbs. Gradually add enough water to form a good consistency. Press into a ball with your hands and chill in the fridge for at least 30 minutes.

Pre-heat the oven to 220°C/425°F/Gas 7. To make the filling, heat the vegetable oil and the butter in a large frying pan and sauté the onions over a fairly high heat for about 5 minutes. Lower the heat and cook for a further 20 minutes, cover with non-stick baking paper, and stir occasionally until the onions are caramelised. Season with a little salt. Lightly beat the eggs, stir in the milk, cream and the grated Gruyère cheese. Season with a little pepper and stir in the caramelised onions.

Grease a 25 x 4 cm (10 x 1½ in) deep loose-bottomed flan tin. On a lightly floured work surface, roll out the dough and line the base and sides of the flan tin. Prick the base of the pastry and bake blind in an oven for 10 minutes. Remove the baking paper and the beans, turn down the temperature to 190°C/375°F/Gas 5 and cook for a further 5 minutes. Spoon the onion mixture into the flan case and sprinkle with the Parmesan cheese. Bake in the oven for 20 to 25 minutes.

The Caramelised Onion and Gruyère Tart is shown overleaf

Vegetable Burgers

These vegetable burgers are delicious eaten either hot or cold.

Makes 8 vegetable burgers

2 medium carrots, grated
1 medium courgette, grated
1 onion, chopped
50 g (2 oz) chestnut or button mushrooms, chopped
75 g (3 oz) cashew nuts, roughly chopped
1 tablespoon chopped fresh oregano or
½ teaspoon dried oregano
1 tablespoon chopped fresh parsley

a pinch of cayenne pepper (optional)
150 g (5 oz) fresh brown breadcrumbs plus
100 g (4 oz) for coating
15 ml (1 tbsp) tomato sauce
7.5 ml (½ tbsp) soy sauce
½ small egg
salt and freshly ground black pepper
vegetable oil for frying

Using your hands, squeeze out some of the excess moisture from the grated carrots and courgette. In a large bowl, mix together the vegetables, cashew nuts, herbs, cayenne pepper and 150 g (5 oz) of the breadcrumbs. Beat together the tomato sauce, soy sauce and the half egg, stir this into the vegetable mixture and season. Using your hands, form the mixture into eight burgers and coat with the remaining breadcrumbs. At this stage you can set the burgers aside in the fridge to firm up, but it is not essential. Sauté the burgers in vegetable oil, turning occasionally until they are golden.

Mashed Potato with Carrot

There are lots of different ways to turn ordinary mashed potatoes into something special. This is one of my favourites. For a really smooth texture you can add a little more butter and milk.

Makes 3 portions

450 g (1 lb) potatoes, peeled and chopped
1 large carrot, thinly sliced
25 g (1 oz) butter

15 ml (1 tbsp) milk
salt and freshly ground black pepper

Put the potatoes and carrot into a pan of lightly salted water. Bring to the boil and then cook for about 20 minutes or until the vegetables are tender. Drain and then mash together with the butter, milk and seasoning until quite smooth. You can make lovely domes of mash using an ice cream scoop.

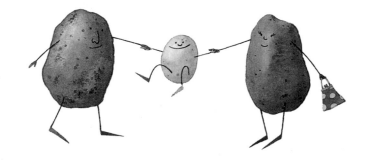

Ratatouille Omelette

This concoction of sautéed Mediterranean vegetables mixed with eggs and topped with grated cheese in the style of a Spanish omelette is quite delicious and a meal in itself. (*See photograph opposite*)

Serves 6

1 aubergine, sliced
1 small onion, sliced
45 ml (3 tbsp) olive oil
1 large courgette, sliced
1 red pepper, cored, de-seeded and cut into strips
2 tomatoes, skinned, de-seeded and chopped
salt and freshly ground black pepper
6 eggs

30 ml (2 tbsp) cold water
25 g (1 oz) butter
75 ml (3 fl oz) double cream
75 g (3 oz) Gruyère cheese, grated

> **MENU PLANNING**
> *Omelettes are the perfect all-in-one lunch.*
> *See Spring Planner, page 10.*

Gently sauté the onion in olive oil in a heavy-based frying pan until soft. Chop the aubergine and add with the courgette and pepper, cover the pan and cook for about 20 minutes or until the vegetables are soft but not mushy. Add the tomatoes and cook for a further 5 minutes. Season to taste.

Lightly whisk the eggs with the cold water, then mix in the cooked vegetables. Heat the butter in a deep 25-cm (10-in) omelette or frying pan. When the butter is frothy, pour the egg mixture into the pan and cook until set. Remove from the heat, pour over the double cream and cover with the grated cheese. Cook under a pre-heated grill for a few minutes until golden. Leave the handle of the frying pan sticking out of the grill and cover with aluminium foil if necessary.

Delicious Vegetable Rissoles

I make fresh breadcrumbs for this recipe by putting 2 slices of wholemeal bread in a food processor.

Makes 12 rissoles

150 g (5 oz) carrots, grated
100 g (4 oz) butternut squash, grated
75 g (3 oz) white of leek, finely chopped
100 g (4 oz) button mushrooms, finely chopped
1 tablespoon freshly chopped parsley

100 g (4 oz) wholemeal breadcrumbs
10 ml (2 tsp) soy sauce
1 egg, lightly beaten
salt and freshly ground black pepper
vegetable oil for frying

In a large bowl, mix the vegetables and parsley together with the breadcrumbs, soy sauce, beaten egg and seasoning. Using your hands, form into about twelve rissoles. Heat the oil in a large frying pan and sauté the rissoles over a medium heat for 8 to 10 minutes, turning occasionally until golden and cooked through.

Brown Rice 'Risotto'

Brown rice is far more nutritious than refined white rice, so it's a good idea to introduce some recipes using brown rice that are tasty and appealing. Here is a recipe for you to try.

Serves 4

225 g (8 oz) easy-cook brown rice
1 onion, chopped
1 garlic clove, crushed
22.5 ml (1½ tbsp) olive oil
600 ml (1 pint) vegetable or chicken stock (see Chicken Soup on page 47) (dilute well if making from a cube so that it is not too salty)
100 g (4 oz) carrots, diced
100 g (4 oz) broccoli, cut into small florets
100 g (4 oz) cauliflower, cut into small florets
100 g (4 oz) courgettes, diced

25 g (1 oz) butter
salt and freshly ground black pepper
15 ml (1 tbsp) soy sauce

> **MENU PLANNING**
> When the nights draw in, serve with meat, chicken, fish or an omelette.. See Autumn and Winter Planners, pages 14 and 16.

Rinse the rice and drain. Sauté the onion and garlic in the olive oil for 3 to 4 minutes, then stir in the rice and cook for 1 minute. Pour in the hot stock, bring to the boil. Reduce the heat, cover and cook for about 45 minutes or until the rice is tender. While the rice is cooking, steam the vegetables for about 6 minutes or until tender but still crisp. This is best done in a two-tier steamer with the carrots on the first level and the remaining vegetables on the tier above. Melt the butter in a frying pan and sauté the vegetables for 2 to 3 minutes. Season lightly with salt and pepper. Mix the vegetables with the cooked rice and mix in the soy sauce.

Yummy Vegetables in Oyster Sauce

Here is a very tasty way to prepare vegetables which may well tempt reluctant vegetable eaters. It also makes a delicious accompaniment to an adult meal.

Makes 3 portions

100 g (4 oz) broccoli, cut into small florets
100 g (4 oz) baby corn, cut in half lengthways
100 g (4 oz) carrots cut into thin strips
15 ml (1 tbsp) vegetable oil
75 g (3 oz) shitake or button mushrooms, sliced

7.5 ml (½ tbsp) sake or sherry
7.5 ml (½ tbsp) soy sauce
15 ml (1 tbsp) oyster sauce
salt and freshly ground black pepper
¼ teaspoon caster sugar

Blanch the broccoli, baby corn and carrots by placing them in a large pan of lightly salted water for about 3 minutes. Drain and then rinse with cold water. Heat the oil in a wok or frying pan, add the mushrooms, broccoli and baby corn and stir-fry for 3 minutes. Add the sake or sherry, soy sauce, oyster sauce, pepper and sugar and continue to stir-fry for 2 to 3 minutes or until the vegetables are tender but still crisp.

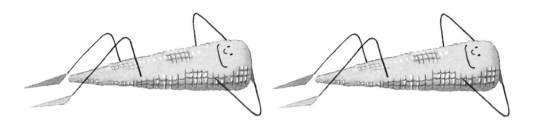

Tomato and Basil Risotto

Risotto is actually very easy to prepare and if you just follow the instructions you can't go wrong. Only use special risotto rice and don't try to cook the rice too quickly. Almost everyone who has eaten this risotto asks me for the recipe – it's a lovely combination of creamy risotto and fresh tomatoes and basil.

Makes 4 portions

2 small or 1 large onion, finely chopped
1 clove garlic, crushed
15 ml (1 tbsp) olive oil
25 g (1 oz) butter
1.25 litres (1¾ pints) good vegetable stock or chicken stock (see Chicken Soup on page 47)
60 ml (4 tbsp) white wine
225 g (7½ oz) arborio (risotto) rice

2 tablespoons chopped sun-dried tomatoes
4 fresh tomatoes (225 g/8 oz), skinned, de-seeded and chopped
40 g (1½ oz) Parmesan cheese, grated
15 g (½ oz) butter
2 tablespoons torn fresh basil leaves, plus extra for serving
freshly ground black pepper

Heat the oil and half the butter in a large frying pan and sauté the onion and garlic until soft. Heat the stock in a saucepan, add the wine and leave it to simmer by the side of the frying pan. Add the rice to the sautéed onion, stir for 1 minute, then add a ladleful of stock and simmer, stirring occasionally, until it has been absorbed. Keep adding stock a ladleful at a time and stir until it has all been absorbed and the rice is cooked al dente (about 25 minutes).

Five minutes before the end, add the chopped dried tomatoes. Then add the fresh tomatoes, Parmesan cheese, the remaining butter and the torn basil leaves and serve with more basil leaves scattered on top. Season with some fresh ground black pepper.

Spotted Snake Pizza

This pizza is great fun to make together with your child. It almost looks too good to eat!

15 g (½ oz) active dried yeast
250 ml (8 fl oz) lukewarm water
a pinch of sugar
30 ml (2 tbsp) olive oil
400 g (14 oz) strong white flour
1 teaspoon salt
75 g (3 oz) Cheddar cheese
1 egg, lightly beaten

Topping
10 tablespoons ready-made tomato sauce with
herbs
200 g (7 oz) Mozzarella cheese, cut into slices
red, orange and yellow mini peppers, cored and
de-seeded
2 black olives, stoned
small piece of green pepper

Place the yeast in a mixing bowl, pour over the warm water, stir in the sugar and mix with a fork. Allow to stand until the yeast has dissolved and starts to foam (about 10 minutes). Stir in the olive oil, mix the flour and salt together and fold half of this mixture into the bowl using a wooden spoon. Gradually mix in three-quarters of the remaining flour, stirring with the spoon until the dough forms a sticky mass and begins to come away from the sides of the bowl.

Sprinkle some of the remaining flour on to a smooth work surface. Remove the dough from the bowl and gradually knead in the remaining flour, a little at a time, until the dough is smooth and elastic and no longer sticks to your hands. This will probably take between 8 and 10 minutes. Form into a ball and place in an oiled bowl, cover with a damp tea-towel and leave in a warm place to rise for about 50 minutes, or until doubled in size. To test whether the dough has risen enough, stick two fingers in the dough and if the indentations remain, the dough is ready. Punch the dough down with your fist and place on a floured work surface. Knead again for a few minutes until the dough is nice and elastic.

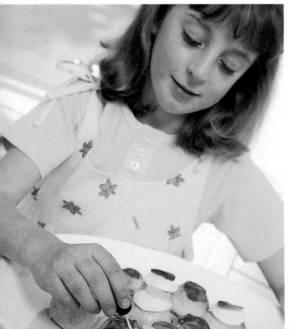

Pre-heat the oven to 200°C/400°F/Gas 6. Divide the dough into about 12 balls with one larger ball for the head of the snake and make a small tail from the dough for the end of the snake. Stuff each of the balls with a small cube of Cheddar cheese, making sure it is completely covered with dough. Place the balls and tail on a large greased baking tray in the shape of a snake so that they are just touching each other. Brush the tops of the balls with beaten egg and cook in the oven for 10 minutes, or until lightly golden and joined together. Top each ball alternately with tomato sauce and a slice of Mozzarella cheese, and decorate with mini sweet pepper shapes, which can be cut out using mini biscuit cutters. Bake for a further 5 minutes. Add olives for eyes and a forked tongue cut out from a strip of green pepper to complete the snake.

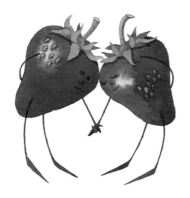

Cakes

Josie's Delicious Carrot Cake

Carrot cake is one of my favourite cakes and Josie is a friend of mine who is always keen to try out my new recipes on her husband and two boys. This is her favourite recipe for carrot cake. I've added the chopped pecans, raisins and marzipan carrots but you can leave these out if you prefer.

Serves 6-8

180 ml (6 fl oz) vegetable oil
175 g (6 oz) soft brown sugar
3 eggs, beaten
150 g (5 oz) plain flour, sieved
1¼ teaspoons baking powder
1¼ teaspoons bicarbonate of soda
1 teaspoon salt
1 teaspoon cinnamon
¼ teaspoon nutmeg
225 g (8 oz) grated carrots
50 g (2 oz) pecans, finely chopped
100 g (4 oz) raisins

Icing
35 g (1½ oz) unsalted butter
130 g (4½ oz) icing sugar, sifted
150 g (5 oz) cream cheese

Marzipan carrots
225 g (8 oz) marzipan
orange and green food colouring

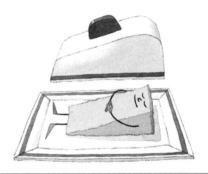

MENU PLANNING
Any of the recipes in this chapter are good for lunchboxes as an added treat.

Pre-heat the oven to 180°C/350°F/Gas 4. Grease and line a 20 cm (8 in) cake tin. Mix the oil and sugar together and add the beaten eggs. Add the flour, baking powder, bicarbonate of soda, salt, cinnamon and nutmeg. Then stir in the grated carrots, pecans and raisins. Put the mixture in the prepared tin and bake in the oven for 50 minutes.

To make the icing, beat together the butter, sugar and vanilla essence – this is best done with a wooden spoon. Stir in the cream cheese until blended, but don't overbeat or the icing will become watery. When the cake is cool, spread the cream cheese frosting evenly over the top of the cake using a palette knife dipped in warm water. Then use a fork to make decorative swirls in the frosting.

To make the marzipan carrots, divide the marzipan into one large and one small ball. Knead some orange food colouring into the larger ball and knead some green food colouring into the smaller ball. Then mould the marzipan into carrots to decorate the cake.

Raspberry and White Chocolate Chip Muffins

The sweet white chocolate chips and the slightly tart taste of the raspberries complement each other beautifully in these delicious, easy-to-prepare muffins. If you can't find white chocolate chips, break-up a white chocolate bar into small pieces. Home-baked muffins also make a lovely gift for friends presented in a wicker basket lined with gingham.

***Makes 6 large
or 8 smaller
muffins***

150 g (5 oz) self-raising flour
1 teaspoon baking powder
a pinch of salt
100 g (4 oz) soft brown sugar
50 g (2 oz) melted butter
1 egg, lightly beaten

125 ml (4 fl oz) milk
2.5 ml (½ tsp) vanilla essence
100 g (4 oz) raspberries
50 g (2 oz) white chocolate chips
½ tablespoon demerera sugar

Pre-heat the oven to 180°C/350°F/Gas 4. Mix together the dry ingredients, lifting with your fingers to incorporate some air. Melt the butter, beat together the egg, milk and vanilla essence and fold the dry ingredients into the wet mixture but do not beat.

Fold the raspberries and white chocolate chips into the mixture. Spoon into muffin cases. Sprinkle the demerera sugar over the muffins. Bake in the oven for 25 minutes until well risen and just firm.

Funny Face Fairy Cakes

These are always very popular at children's birthday parties, decorated with faces made from a mixture of small sweets and writing icing. My children adore making their own funny faces. You can also make miniature fairy cakes for young children using paper cases for confectionery and baking the cakes in a mini-muffin tin.

Makes 10 cupcakes

100 g (4 oz) self-raising flour
100 g (4 oz) soft margarine
100 g (4 oz) caster sugar
2 eggs
5 ml (1 tsp) vanilla essence
1 teaspoon grated lemon rind
75 g (3 oz) raisins or sultanas (optional)

Icing
175 g (6 oz) icing sugar, sifted
water
small tubes of coloured writing icing
Liquorice Allsorts, Dolly Mixtures, Smarties,
Jelly Tots

Pre-heat the oven to 180°C/350°F/Gas 4. Put the larger paper cases in a bun tray and the sweet cases in a mini-muffin tray. Sieve the self-raising flour into a mixing bowl. Add the margarine, caster sugar and eggs and beat everything together until the mixture is soft and creamy. Beat in the vanilla essence and grated lemon rind. If you don't want to decorate the fairy cakes, you could make plump raisin or sultana cupcakes by folding raisins or sultanas into the batter at this stage.

Spoon the batter into the cases until about two-thirds full. Bake the larger cakes in the oven for about 20 minutes, and the smaller cakes for about 12 minutes or until a cocktail stick inserted into the centre comes out clean. Turn them on to a wire rack to cool.

To make the icing, sift the icing sugar into a bowl and gradually stir in a little water to make a thick smooth paste. Once the cakes are cool, ice and decorate them.

Upside-down Banana Cake

Makes 8 portions

175 g (6 oz) self-raising flour
a pinch of salt
1 medium banana, mashed
30 ml (2 tbsp) crème fraîche
5 ml (1 tsp) vanilla essence
175 g (6 oz) caster sugar
75 g (3 oz) unsalted butter, softened
2 eggs, lightly beaten

Base/topping
75 g (3 oz) light brown sugar
75 g (3 oz) unsalted butter, softened
2 to 3 bananas

Pre-heat the oven to 180°C/350°F/Gas 4. Sift the flour and salt into a bowl. In a separate bowl, mix the mashed banana with the crème fraîche and vanilla essence.

Cream the sugar and butter until light and fluffy, then beat in the eggs, a little at a time. Now fold in the flour and banana mixture alternately, stirring until thoroughly combined.

To make the base/topping, cream the sugar and butter until light and fluffy and smear over the base and a little way up the sides of a heavy-based oven-proof pan about 25 cm (10 in) in diameter and 5 cm (2 in) deep. Slice the bananas and arrange over the base.

Spoon over the sponge mixture, smoothing the top. Bake in the oven for 45 to 50 minutes or until the sponge is golden brown on top and feels slightly springy to the touch.

Leave to cook in the dish for about 5 to 10 minutes, then turn upside down on to a large serving dish. Serve warm.

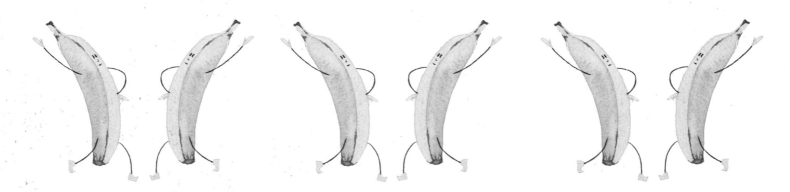

Nathalie's Chocolate Chip Cake

Nathalie is a good friend of mine who lives in my street, which is handy if I run out of things like eggs, which I do all the time! Sheís a super cook and a mother of 10-year-old twin boys and a little girl of 5 years. This is a recipe handed down by her grandmother, who used to meticulously measure all the ingredients in tablespoons. It's a delicious, foolproof recipe, which takes less than 10 minutes to prepare.

Makes 6-8 cakes

15 g (½ oz) brown sugar
100 g (4 oz) unsalted butter at room temperature
2 eggs

100 g (4 oz) self-raising flour
5 ml (1 tsp) vanilla sugar
1 teaspoon baking powder
100 g (4 oz) good quality plain chocolate

Pre-heat the oven to 170°C/325°F/Gas 3 and butter and flour a non-stick 18 cm (7 in) diameter cake tin. Cream the butter and sugar in a food processor. Add one egg and half the quantity of flour and blend in the processor. Add the vanilla sugar, baking powder, the rest of the flour and the other egg. Mix again until well blended.

Break the chocolate into pieces and put in the processor. Process briefly (3-4 seconds) until chocolate is broken into smallish pieces. Pour into the prepared tin and place in the oven for about 30-35 minutes.

SWEET FOODS AND TOOTH DECAY

It is the frequency with which sweet foods are eaten that does the most damage to your child's teeth. If your child is eating sugar or drinking fruit juices continually throughout a prolonged period there will be little chance for saliva to prevent bacteria around the gums turning sugar into acids that attack the teeth's enamel. It is much better to allow your child to eat sweets all in one go so that the mouth can return to a neutral balance.

Tucking into a stick of celery or some grapes with cheese will also help to produce acid that prevents tooth decay. Finishing a meal with some cheese or giving cheese as a snack between meals helps to protect your child's teeth from decay. Cheese contains fat and salt to stimulate acid-neutralising saliva and a combination of calcium and a milk protein, which speeds up natural repairs to the surface of the teeth. Cheese is also effective against acid from fruit, juices and soft drinks. Try to limit sweet foods to mealtimes and try to encourage young children to enjoy eating healthy snacks like those listed below:

- Bread and sandwiches
- Savoury biscuits, such as rice cakes, crisp bread, cheese biscuits
- Cheese
- Raw vegetables with a dip or salads
- Natural yoghurt with fruit and a little honey

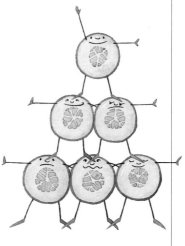

Annabel's Apricot Cookies

This fabulous and rather unusual combination of dried apricots and white chocolate makes irresistible cookies. Once you have sampled these you will probably want to double the quantities second time around. (*See photograph opposite*)

Makes 26 cookies

100 g (4 oz) unsalted butter
100 g (4 oz) cream cheese
100 g (4 oz) caster sugar
75 g (3 oz) plain flour
50 g (2 oz) chopped dried apricots
65 g (2½ oz) white chocolate chips or chopped
white chocolate

MENU PLANNING
Cookies need not only be eaten on their own
– they make a good dessert too.

Pre-heat the oven to 180°C/350°F/Gas 4. In a large mixing bowl, cream together the butter and cream cheese. Add the sugar and beat until fluffy. Gradually add the flour, then fold in the apricots and chocolate. The dough will be quite soft – don't worry! Drop the mixture by heaped teaspoons on to baking sheets lined with non-stick baking paper and bake in the oven for 15 minutes or until lightly golden. Allow to cool and harden for a few minutes before removing them from the baking sheet.

Apricot and Coconut Muffins

Everyone in the family will love these delicious moist muffins. Serve plain or, for a special occasion, warm some apricot jam with a little water, brush this over the tops of the muffins, sprinkle over a little desiccated coconut and stick a glacé cherry on top.

Makes 10 muffins

2 eggs, lightly beaten
125 ml (4 fl oz) vegetable oil
1 x 125 ml (4 fl oz) can of crushed pineapple
in natural juice
50 g (2 oz) dried apricots, finely chopped
75 g (3 oz) caster sugar

25 g (1 oz) desiccated coconut
100 g (4 oz) plain flour
½ tablespoon baking powder
a pinch of baking soda
a pinch of salt

Pre-heat the oven to 180°C/350°F/Gas 4. In a large bowl, mix together the first six ingredients. Sift together the flour, baking powder, baking soda and salt and fold these into the first mixture (do not over-mix). Line a muffin tray with paper cases, pour in the batter and bake in the oven for 25–30 minutes.

Coffee and Walnut Gâteau

Coffee essence adds a delicious flavour to this cake. However, you could substitute 10 ml (2 tsp) of instant coffee mixed with 15 ml (1 tbsp) of hot water. This is very simple to prepare as all the ingredients for the cake are put into one bowl and mixed together.

Makes 8-10 portions

50 g (2 oz) walnuts, finely chopped
175 g (6 oz) soft margarine
100 g (4 oz) caster sugar
50 g (2 oz) light muscovado sugar
175 g (6 oz) self-raising flour
1 teaspoon baking powder
3 eggs, lightly beaten
15 ml (1 tbsp) coffee essence

Icing

75 g (3 oz) soft margarine
225 g (8 oz) icing sugar, sieved
10 ml (2 tsp) milk
10 ml (2 tsp) coffee essence

50 g (2 oz) caster sugar
50 g (2 oz) walnut halves

Pre-heat the oven to 160°C/325°F/Gas 3. Grease and line the bases of two 20 cm (8 in) sandwich tins. Put the chopped nuts, margarine, sugars, flour, baking powder, eggs and coffee essence into a large bowl and beat together until thoroughly blended. Divide the mixture evenly between the two tins and level the surface. Bake for 25 to 30 minutes or until the cakes are risen and golden and the cakes spring back when lightly pressed down with your fingers. Leave to cool for a few minutes, then turn out, peel off the paper and set aside on a wire rack.

Meanwhile, to prepare the icing, beat together the margarine, icing sugar, milk and coffee essence until smooth.

To finish off you can prepare some caramelised walnuts for the topping. Put the caster sugar into a small heavy-based saucepan and stir until dissolved. Continue to cook without stirring until the mixture turns a light golden brown (watch carefully as this can burn very quickly). Remove from the heat and toss the walnuts in the caramel, then spread them on to a greased baking sheet to allow the caramel to set.

When the cakes are completely cold, sandwich them together with half of the icing and use the rest for the top of the cake. Decorate with the caramelised walnuts.

Apple and Sultana Cake

This is a lovely, moist, old-fashioned apple cake. I find that cooking apples have a much better flavour than eating apples, but don't be tempted to add more apple or the cake will become soggy.

Makes 10 portions

3 medium eggs
200 ml (6½ fl oz) sunflower oil
225 g (8 oz) brown sugar
50 ml (2 fl oz) cold water
325 g (11 oz) plain flour
50 g (2 oz) desiccated coconut
½ teaspoon salt
1 teaspoon bicarbonate of soda
1½ teaspoons mixed spice
10 ml (2 tsp) vanilla essence

1 large cooking apple (about 400 g/14 oz), peeled and chopped
150 g (5 oz) sultanas
75 g (3 oz) pecans, chopped (optional)

Butterscotch topping
50 g (2 oz) light muscovado sugar
30 ml (2 tbsp) milk
50 g (2 oz) butter

Pre-heat the oven to 180°C/350°F/Gas 4. Whisk together the eggs, oil, sugar and water. Sift together the flour, salt, bicarbonate of soda and mixed spice and fold this into the egg mixture. Add the vanilla essence, coconut, chopped apples, sultanas and pecans, if using.

Line the base of a 25 cm (10 in) tin and grease the sides, then pour in the mixture. Place in the oven and bake for about 1 hour or until a wooden skewer inserted in the middle comes out clean. If the top of the cake looks as though it is getting too brown towards the end of the cooking time, cover it loosely with aluminium foil.

Place the ingredients for the sauce in a pan and bring slowly to the boil. Boil for about 4 minutes, stirring until thickened. Allow to cool. Once the cake is cooked, remove from the oven and pour the sauce over the top. Return to the oven and bake for another 2 minutes. Allow to cool in the tin and then remove.

Annabel's No-bake Train Cake

The beauty of this cake is that it requires no cooking and can be created in very little time from basic ready-made ingredients. Older children will enjoy helping you assemble it but watch out that they don't eat the ingredients first as it's made out of all the things that children love. You can choose any selection of sweets for the goods carriages.

Serves 20

Grass
2 x 250 g (8½ oz) packets desiccated coconut
1 x 38 ml (1½ oz) edible green food colouring
water
75 ml (5 tbsp) apricot jam

Chocolate buttercream
75 g (3 oz) butter, softened
125 g (4½ oz) icing sugar
1 tablespoon cocoa powder
15 ml (1 tbsp) milk

5 x 205 g (7 oz) large chocolate-covered swiss
roll filled with chocolate buttercream
1 milk chocolate marshmallow tea cake

1 chocolate Rolo
1 x 227 g (8 oz) packet Liquorice Allsorts
1 packet of liquorice catherine wheels
1 box chocolate sticks
1 x 150 g (5 oz) box white chocolate fingers
1 x 150 g (5 oz) box milk chocolate fingers
20 milk chocolate-coated mini swiss rolls
6 raspberry jam sandwich creams

1 x 150 g (5 oz) packet of fizzy strawberry
and cream flavour lances
1 x 100 g (4 oz) packet Dolly Mixtures
1 x 200 g (7 oz) packet mini marshmallows
2 mini packets assorted sweets

To make the grass to cover the cake board, thoroughly mix the desiccated coconut with a little of the green food colouring and a few drops of water. Warm the apricot jam and brush it over the surface of two 40 x 30 cm (16 x 12 in) silver cake boards. The cake boards can be stuck together first if you like or if you are going to transport the cake, it's probably best if they are left separate. Strew the green coconut over the cake boards and press down on to the board so that they are completely covered.

To make the chocolate buttercream, beat the softened butter until creamy. Sift the icing sugar and cocoa powder into the bowl and beat together with the butter. Finally, beat in the milk. Cut about 5 cm (2 in) off the end of one of the large chocolate swiss rolls and secure this on top of a whole large chocolate Swiss roll to form the engine with some of the chocolate buttercream or a cocktail stick to form the cab. Secure a chocolate marshmallow tea cake with a Rolo to form the chimney. Attach two Liquorice Allsorts to form the windows of the cab. Attach a liquorice catherine wheel to the front of the cab with some of the buttercream. If you like, attach cotton wool balls on to a length of wire to look like steam coming from the engine.

Annabel's No-bake Train Cake is shown overleaf

Lay out the track using two parallel lines of chocolate sticks in a zigzag pattern and lay white chocolate and milk chocolate fingers alternately across the track to form the railway line. You will need to allow for the engine and five carriages. Put five mini milk chocolate rolls at the front of the track to form the bumper and the wheels of the engine and balance the engine on top. Attach three raspberry sandwich cream biscuits to each side of the engine with some of the buttercream to form the wheels and decorate the front with three Liquorice Allsorts. Cut a thin slice off the top of the remaining large chocolate Swiss rolls to form the carriages of the train and spread the flat surfaces with some of the chocolate buttercream. Lay each of the carriages over the mini swiss rolls along the track. Pile the sweets on to the open trucks.

Coconut Kisses

I defy you to eat only one of these! They're definitely one of my favourites, and your children will enjoy helping you make as well as eat them.

Makes 25 biscuits

100 g (4 oz) butter
50 g (2 oz) soft brown sugar
50 g (2 oz) caster sugar
1 egg, beaten
2.5 ml (½ tsp) pure vanilla extract
75 g (3 oz) plain flour
½ teaspoon baking soda
½ teaspoon salt
120 g (4½ oz) plain chocolate chips
75 g (3 oz) rolled oats
40 g (1½ oz) desiccated coconut

MENU PLANNING
Serve with ice cream for an unusual combination.
See Spring Planner, page 10.

Pre-heat the oven to 180°C/350°F/Gas 4. Cream together the butter and sugars. Add the egg and vanilla. Sift together the flour, baking soda and salt and beat this into the mixture. Stir in the chocolate chips, oats and coconut. Form into walnut-sized balls, flatten the top with your hand and place spaced apart on a lightly greased or lined baking tray. Bake in the oven for 10–15 minutes. The biscuits will harden when they cool down.

Strawberry Cream Cake

A simple and quick cake to make – and it's sure to be a great favourite with everyone in the family.

Makes 8 portions

175 g (6 oz) soft margarine
175 g (6 oz) soft brown sugar
3 large eggs, beaten
175 g (6 oz) self-raising flour
½ teaspoon lemon zest
5 ml (1 tsp) vanilla essence
15 ml (1 tbsp) water

Filling/topping
300 ml (½ pint) whipping or double cream
3 tablespoons icing sugar
150 g (6 oz) strawberries
30-45 ml (2-3 tbsp) strawberry jam

Pre-heat the oven to 180°C/350°F/Gas 4 and line and grease two 20 cm (8 in) sandwich tins. Beat together the margarine and sugar, then add the eggs, one at a time, adding 1 tablespoon of flour with the eggs after the first egg to stop the mixture from curdling. Beat in the remaining flour, the lemon zest, vanilla essence and water until light and fluffy.

Divide the mixture between the prepared sandwich tins and bake in the oven for about 20 minutes or until lightly golden and risen. Turn them out of the tins and put on a wire rack to cool.

Whip the cream with the icing sugar until firm. Thinly slice 100 g (4 oz) of the strawberries. Stir the strawberries into two-thirds of the whipped cream. Spread the strawberry jam over one of the cakes, top with the strawberries and cream mixture and place the other cake on top. Using the remaining cream, pipe rosettes around the cake and place half a strawberry on top of each rosette. Keep refrigerated until ready to serve.

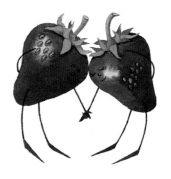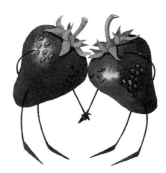

Poppy Seed and Almond Cake

Dark poppy seeds add lovely texture and flavour to this moist almond sponge cake.

*Makes 6-8
portions*

150 g (5 oz) butter
155 g (5 oz) granulated sugar
2 large eggs
150 g (5 oz) self-raising flour
50 g (2 oz) ground almonds

1 teaspoon grated lemon rind
4 ml (¾ tsp) almond essence
30 ml (2 tbsp) very hot water
1 tablespoon poppy seeds

Pre-heat the oven to 180°C/350°F/Gas 4. Grease and line the base of an 18 cm (7 in) loose-bottomed round cake tin. Beat the butter and sugar together until light and fluffy. Beat in the eggs one at a time, adding a tablespoon of the flour with the second egg to stop the mixture from curdling. Sift in the flour and the ground almonds, add the lemon rind and almond essence and fold into the mixture. Finally, stir in the hot water and half the poppy seeds. Spoon the mixture into the prepared tin, level the top and sprinkle with the remaining seeds. Bake in the oven for about 50 minutes or until a skewer inserted in the centre of the cake comes out clean. Remove from the tin and allow to cool on a wire rack.

Best-ever Oatmeal Raisin Cookies

These are my favourite home-made biscuits. Mummy and Daddy gobble them up before the children get a look in!

*Makes about 15
cookies*

75 g (3 oz) butter or margarine
40 g (1½ oz) brown sugar
25 g (1 oz) granulated sugar
½ beaten egg
15 ml (1 tbsp) water
5 ml (1 tsp) vanilla essence
40 g (1½ oz) plain wholemeal flour
½ teaspoon cinnamon or mixed spice
a pinch of salt
¼ teaspoon bicarbonate of soda

75 g (3 oz) oat flakes or quick-cooking rolled
oats
75 g (3 oz) raisins

> **MENU PLANNING**
> *Don't forget these at lunch time – very
> yummy after chicken drumsticks and baked
> potatoes.*
> *See Winter Planner, page 16.*

Pre-heat the oven to 180°C/350°F/Gas 4. Cream the butter or margarine with the sugars. Beat in the egg and add the water and vanilla essence. Sift together the flour, mixed spice, salt and bicarbonate of soda. Mix this into the egg mixture. Finally, stir in the oats and raisins. Line 3 baking sheets with non-stick baking paper. Make walnut-sized balls of dough and flatten these down on to the baking sheet – you may want to enlist the 'help' of your child for this stage. Bake for about 15 minutes, until the edges are done but the centres are still soft.

Apple Smiles

This snack is easy to prepare and will certainly bring a smile to your child's face! For a healthier variation, use small cubes of cheese instead of mini marshmallows. (*See photograph opposite*)

Makes 4 apple smiles

1 red apple, cored and sliced into eighths
a squeeze of lemon juice
smooth peanut butter

miniature marshmallows or small cubes of cheese (for a healthier alternative)
dried apricots (optional)

Spread peanut butter on one side of each apple slice (squeeze a little lemon juice over the apple if not serving immediately). Place four miniature marshmallows or cubes of cheese on one apple slice and then lay another apple slice peanut butter side down on top. If you like, add an apricot to form the tongue.

Divinely Decadent Fruity Dark Chocolate Bars

These no-bake chocolate fruit and nut bars are amazingly good and one of my favourite treats. Indulge yourself and make sure they're hidden when Daddy or Mummy comes home. They are also fun for children to make themselves.

Makes 12 bars

300 g (10 oz) good quality plain chocolate
100 g (4 oz) unsalted butter
225 g (8 oz) digestive biscuits
1 x 397 g (14 oz) can of condensed milk

100 g (4 oz) no-soak dried peaches (or apricots), chopped
50 g (2 oz) raisins
75 g (3 oz) pecans, roughly chopped

Break the chocolate into squares and cut the butter into pieces, put these into a large bowl and place over a saucepan of simmering water, stirring occasionally until melted. Break the biscuits into pieces. Then stir the condensed milk into the chocolate mixture and mix in the broken biscuits, chopped peaches or apricots, raisins and chopped pecans.

Line an 18 x 28 cm (7 x 11 in) shallow cake tin with clear film allowing the sides to overhang. Spoon the mixture into the tin and press down but still leaving the top a little rough. Set aside in the fridge to set. Once set, lift the cake out of the tin by the overhanging clear film and cut into bars. Keep chilled in the fridge.

Glossy Dark and White Chocolate Brownies

Two chocolates are combined to make these irresistible squares of rich, chewy brownies. (*See photograph opposite*)

**Makes 16
squares**

150 g (5 oz) dark chocolate, chopped
75 g (3 oz) unsalted butter
5 ml (1 tsp) pure vanilla extract
100 g (4 oz) caster sugar
2 eggs
1 egg yolk
90 g (3½ oz) plain flour
¼ teaspoon salt

150 g (5 oz) white chocolate buttons or
chipped white chocolate

Chocolate satin glaze
75 g (3 oz) dark chocolate, chopped
15 g (½ oz) unsalted butter
50 g (2 oz) white chocolate buttons

Pre-heat the oven to 180°C/350°F/Gas 4 and line and grease a 20 cm (8 in) square baking pan. Melt the dark chocolate and butter in a microwave for 2 minutes on High (or in a saucepan over a gentle heat, stirring constantly). Stir in the vanilla and sugar, then add the eggs and yolk, one at a time, stirring after each addition. Sift together the flour and salt and mix this into the chocolate mixture with the chopped white chocolate. Pour the batter into the prepared pan and bake in the oven for about 30 minutes.

To prepare the glaze, melt the dark chocolate and butter together and spread over the cake. Melt the white chocolate buttons and using a teaspoon trail 5 lines horizontally across the cake about 1 cm (½ in) apart. With a blunt knife draw vertical lines lightly through the chocolate topping to create a pattern.

Mars Bar and Rice Crispies Slice

These are very popular for parties and no one will know what they are made from if you don't tell them! They will keep for one week if they are not gobbled up sooner!

Makes 20 slices

3 x 65 g (1½ oz) Mars Bars
90 g (3½ oz) butter
75 g (3 oz) Rice Crispies

Topping
200 g (7 oz) plain chocolate
25 g (1 oz) butter

Grease a 28 x 18 cm (11 x 7 in) shallow tin. Melt the Mars Bars and butter in a saucepan, stirring occasionally (don't boil). Stir in the Rice Crispies. Press into the tin and set aside in the fridge to set for about 1 hour. For the topping, put the chocolate and butter in a saucepan and heat gently, stirring occasionally until melted. Spread the topping over the Rice Crispie mixture and when cool, put in the fridge to set. With a sharp knife, cut into 20 bars.

Desserts

Caramelised Almond Ice Cream

This ice cream tastes sensational, is very simple to make and you don't need to use an ice cream machine. As a variation this is also very good using pecans instead of almonds. It goes well with fresh peaches, which can be served hot with some ice cream on the side. Simply wash and stone the peaches, cut in half, and sprinkle with a little brown sugar. Place under a pre-heated grill for a few minutes.

Serves 6

1 x 410 g (14 oz) can of evaporated milk

Caramelised almonds
225 g (8 oz) blanched almonds
225 g (8 oz) soft brown sugar

45 ml (3 tbsp) cold water
150 g (5 oz) caster sugar
300 ml (½ pint) double cream
10 ml (2 tsp) vanilla essence

Chill the can of evaporated milk in the freezer for about 3 hours. For the caramelised almonds, toast the almonds under a pre-heated grill for a few minutes until golden, turning once. Put the sugar into a heavy-bottomed saucepan together with the water and cook, stirring, over a gentle heat until it caramelises. Stir in the almonds and coat with the sticky caramel. Transfer to a baking tray to cool down.

Once cool, place the caramelised almonds in a tea towel, wrap up and crush with a mallet or rolling pin. Whip the frozen milk with the caster sugar until thick. Whip the double cream and mix into the evaporated milk mixture together with the vanilla essence and the crushed almonds. Put into a suitable container and freeze.

Summer Fruit Brulée with Amaretto Biscuits

This is one of my favourite desserts and is particularly good in summer when peaches and berry fruits are in season. You can also make this using other combinations of fruits – but it's important that the fruit should be really ripe and have a good flavour. Fruits that work well are mangoes, grapes, nectarines, strawberries, kiwis, and you could mix in some passion fruit pulp if you like.

Makes 6 portions

150 g (5 oz) blueberries
150 g (5 oz) raspberries
2 ripe juicy peaches, peeled and chopped

50 g (2 oz) amaretto biscuits, crushed
300 ml (½ pint) crème fraîche
1½ tablespoons light muscovado sugar

Mix the fruit together and arrange in an oven-proof dish. Sprinkle the crushed amaretto biscuits on top and pour over the crème fraîche. Set aside in the fridge for at least 1 hour. Sprinkle over the brown sugar and place under a pre-heated grill for a few minutes until golden.

Louise's Apple and Blackberry Pudding

Louise is a good friend of mine who has two children, Olivia and Ben, both of whom are very fussy eaters. This is one of her children's favourite desserts and it's quick and easy to make. Blackberries are rich in vitamin C and my children love them. Here the slightly tart flavour of the fruit blends really well with the almond sponge topping. Serve hot on its own or with custard or vanilla ice cream.

Serves 4

100 g (4 oz) butter
100 g (4 oz) caster sugar
2 eggs
100 g (4 oz) ground almonds
5 ml (1 tsp) almond essence
450 g (1 lb) cooking apples, peeled and sliced
225 g (8 oz) blackberries, fresh or frozen

> **MENU PLANNING**
> *Particularly good after lasagne or fish fingers and chips.*
> *See Autumn and Winter Planners, pages 14 and 16.*

Pre-heat the oven to 170°C/325°F/Gas 3. Cream together the butter and sugar and beat in the eggs, ground almonds and almond essence. Mix together the fruit and place in an oven-proof dish. Spread the topping over the fruit and bake in the oven for 45 minutes.

Very Easy Raspberry Mousse

This can be made with any fruit – using either fresh or canned works well. It is also good using orange jelly and a can of mandarins or strawberry jelly and fresh strawberries.

Makes 6 portions

1 x 400 g (14 oz) can of raspberries
1 x 135 g (4½ oz) packet of raspberry jelly

1 x 410g (14 oz) can of evaporated milk

Strain the juice from the can of raspberries and make up to 300 ml (½ pint) of liquid with some water. Cut the jelly into cubes and put into a saucepan together with the raspberry liquid. Stir over a medium heat until the jelly has dissolved. Pour into a deep bowl to cool.

When partially set, whisk in the evaporated milk and stir in the raspberries. Set aside in the fridge to set. This looks fun if you layer the mousse with some fresh berries in tall glasses.

Desert Island Pineapple

Here is a very attractive way to serve fresh fruit for a special occasion. (*See photograph opposite*)

Serves 6

1 large pineapple
assorted fruit,
such as strawberries, blueberries,
raspberries
white grapes

MENU PLANNING
Both of these recipes are very refreshing on a hot summer's day. See Summer Planner, page 12.

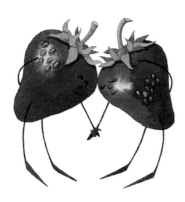

Choose a large pineapple with attractive-looking leaves. Cut the base flat and peel the pineapple, leaving some peel at the bottom to make a steady base for the tree. With a sharp knife, remove the flesh, leaving the hard core to form the trunk of the tree, but leave some of the flesh around the base.

Place the palm tree on a flat plate and arrange the fresh chunks of pineapple around it together with the assorted fresh fruits and decorate the palm tree with the white grapes – small bunches can be tied to the tree with a length of string.

Forest Fruit Lollies

What child can resist an ice lolly, so why not make sure it is made from healthy ingredients? You could also make two-tone ice lollies by filling the lolly moulds half full with the forest fruit mixture and when that has frozen pouring on top a favourite fresh fruit juice of a contrasting colour like passion fruit or apple and mango juice.

Makes 4 lollies

50 g (2 oz) raspberries
50 g (2 oz) strawberries
50 g (2 oz) blueberries

50 g (2 oz) blackberries
1½ to 2 tablespoons icing sugar, sieved
1 x 150 g (5 oz) pot of raspberry yoghurt

Put the berries into a saucepan together with the icing sugar and cook over a gentle heat for a few minutes until the fruit is soft and mushy. Purée the fruit and sieve, then stir in the yoghurt. Pour into ice-lolly moulds and freeze.

Auntie Ruthie's Quick and Easy Cheesecake

It will be hard to beat the taste of this delicious cheesecake and it's very quick and simple to prepare. Serve it plain or with the fresh strawberry topping. For best results use a good quality fresh cream cheese.

Serves 6

225 g (7½ oz) digestive biscuits
125 g (4½ oz) butter

600 g (1 lb 5 oz) cream cheese
150 g (5 oz) caster sugar
2 large eggs
5 ml (1 tsp) vanilla essence
600 ml (1 pint) sour cream
2 tablespoons granulated sugar

Strawberry topping
550 g (1¼ lb) strawberries
45 ml (3 tbsp) seedless raspberry jam

Pre-heat the oven to 180°C/350°F/Gas 4. To make the base, crush the digestive biscuits. This can be done by breaking up the biscuits, putting them in a large plastic bag and crushing them with a rolling pin or alternatively break them up in a food processor. Melt the butter and stir the melted butter into the crushed biscuits.

Line the base and grease a 23 cm (9 in) loose-bottomed cake tin and spoon the crumbs over the base, pressing down well (a potato masher is useful for this). In a food processor, beat together the cream cheese, sugar, eggs, vanilla essence and half the sour cream. Pour the cream cheese mixture over the biscuit base and bake in the oven for 25 minutes. Pour over the remaining sour cream mixed with the granulated sugar and then bake for a further 15 minutes.

While the cake is baking in the oven, you can prepare the topping. Spread the raspberry jam in a baking dish and arrange 225 g (8 oz) of halved strawberries on top. Cover with foil and cook at 180°C/350°F/Gas 4 for 20 minutes. Drain the sauce and discard the cooked strawberries. Simmer the sauce in a small saucepan until syrupy. Arrange the remaining strawberries on top of the cake and brush with the syrup.

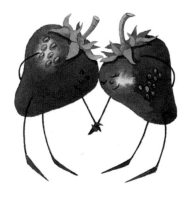

Tiramisu

This popular Italian dessert known as a 'pick me up' is quick and easy to make and is a great way to end a meal. Since this dessert contains raw eggs it should not be eaten by young children.

Makes 6 servings

3 eggs
100 g (4 oz) caster sugar
52.5 ml (3½ tbsp) Marsala wine
400 g (14 oz) Mascarpone cheese

a pinch of salt
250 ml (8 fl oz) strong coffee
24 boudoir biscuits
1 tablespoon cocoa powder

Separate the eggs, put the yolks into a mixing bowl and two of the egg whites into another bowl. Add the sugar to the egg yolks and beat until thick and creamy. Stir in the Marsala and the Mascarpone cheese and mix together with the beaten yolks. Add a pinch of salt to the egg whites and beat until they form stiff peaks. Fold the egg whites into the first mixture until combined. Choose a rectangular dish in which to serve the Tiramisu or prepare individual portions. Pour the coffee into a shallow bowl and dip the boudoir biscuits into the coffee one at a time so that they absorb some of the liquid.

Arrange half the biscuits on the base of the dish, cover with half the Mascarpone mixture, then spoon the remaining Mascarpone mixture on top. Sprinkle the surface with cocoa powder – this is best done using a sieve. Set aside in the fridge for about 4 hours before serving.

Jelly Baby

Jelly is probably one of the most popular children's desserts ever invented. It is delicious served with vanilla ice cream.

Makes 8 servings

2 x 135 g (4½ oz) packets of
blackcurrant jelly
1 x 425 g (15 oz) can of pitted black cherries

100 g (4 oz) fresh or frozen blackcurrants
100 g (4 oz) fresh or frozen blueberries

Break the jelly into squares and place in a large measuring jug. Pour in boiling water up to the 600 ml (1 pint) mark and stir until dissolved. Stir in 450 ml (3/4 pint) of cold water. Drain the cherries and add to the jelly together with the fresh blackcurrants and blueberries. Pour into a mould or serving dish and, when cool, put in the fridge to set.

Chocolate Banana Pancakes

My son Nicholas loves these. He likes to spread the sauce over the pancakes and then roll them up like a swiss roll.
These pancakes are also good with fresh orange segments or raspberries as well as the sliced bananas.

Makes 8 pancakes

100 g (4 oz) plain flour
¼ teaspoon salt
1 tablespoon cocoa powder
1 tablespoon caster sugar
2 eggs, lightly beaten
180 ml (6 fl oz) milk
60 ml (4 tbsp) water
30 ml (2 tbsp) melted butter
a little orange zest (optional)
4 small bananas, sliced, or 2 bananas and
some orange segments or fresh raspberries

Toffee sauce
50 g (2 oz) butter
50 g (2 oz) light brown sugar
50 ml (2 fl oz) double cream
30 ml (2 tbsp) golden syrup

MENU PLANNING
Spaghetti followed by pancakes – every
child's favourite combination.
See Winter Planner, page 16.

Sift the flour, salt, cocoa powder and sugar into a bowl. Make a well in the centre and add the eggs and half the milk. Using a whisk, beat together the ingredients until smooth. Whisk in the rest of the milk and water to make a smooth batter, then stir in the butter and orange zest. This can be set aside in the fridge for up to 30 minutes if you like. Allow to cool down a little and then stir in the cream.

To make the pancakes, brush a heavy-based 18 or 20 cm (7 or 8 in) frying pan with melted butter and when hot ladle in some of the batter and swirl around the frying pan to form a thin layer. Cook for a minute or so on each side.

To make the toffee sauce, place the butter, sugar, cream and golden syrup in a pan. Heat gently until melted then bring to the boil and bubble for 1 minute. Spoon the fruit on to one side of the pancake, drizzle over some of the sauce, fold over in half and then in quarters and spoon over some of the toffee sauce.

Evelyn's Lokshen Pudding

This is a favourite pudding that my mother used to make when I was a child. I now make it for my son Nicholas, who loves it just as much as I did – if not more so.

Makes 6 portions

225 g (8 oz) vermicelli (lokshen)
2 eggs
45 ml (3 tbsp) double cream
2 heaped tablespoons caster sugar
2.5 ml (½ tsp) vanilla essence
50 g (2 oz) each raisins and sultanas
1 teaspoon brown sugar
½ teaspoon cinnamon

a generous knob of butter

> **MENU PLANNING**
> *This is the perfect warming dessert for the autumn and winter months. See Autumn and Winter Planners, pages 14 and 16.*

Pre-heat the oven to 180°C/350°F/Gas 4 and thoroughly butter a fairly shallow dish. Cook the vermicelli in a large pan of lightly salted water according to the instructions on the packet. When cooked, wash well under cold water. Beat the eggs well, add the cream, sugar, vanilla essence, raisins and sultanas. Fold in the lokshen and bake in the prepared dish. Sprinkle with the brown sugar and cinnamon and dot the top with a little butter. Bake in the oven for 35 minutes.

Apple and Plum Crumble

A really good crumble bursting with fruit is comfort food at its very best. Other good fruit fillings are rhubarb, gooseberry, blackberry and apple or strawberry and plum. Serve hot with vanilla ice cream or custard.

Makes 6 portions

780 g (1¾ lb) cooking apples, peeled and cut into chunks
50 g (2 oz) dark brown sugar
4 large ripe plums, stoned and cut into slices

Topping
150 g (5 oz) plain flour
a pinch of salt
90 g (3½ oz) cold butter, cut into pieces
75 g (3 oz) soft brown sugar
50 g (2 oz) rolled oats

Pre-heat the oven to 200°C/400°F/Gas 6. Put the apples into a saucepan with the sugar and cook over a gentle heat for 5-6 minutes, add the quartered plums and cook for 1 minute more. To make the crumble topping, mix together the flour and salt and rub in the butter with your fingers to resemble breadcrumbs. Stir in the sugar and oats. Spoon the fruit into a fairly deep oven-proof dish (I use a dish that measures approximately 25 x 20 cm/10 x 8 in) and cover with the crumble mixture. Bake in the oven for 30 minutes.

Frozen Yoghurt Ice Cream

It takes no time to whip up this creamy yoghurt ice cream and have it in the freezer as a delicious standby. You can choose any flavour yoghurt, I have tried this with cherry yoghurt, mixed berries and also toffee yoghurt. It's great served with fresh fruit and maybe layered in tall glasses with scoops of yoghurt ice and fruit like a knickerbocker glory.

Makes 8 portions

250 ml (8 fl oz) whipping or double cream
180 ml (6 fl oz) condensed milk

5 x 125 g (4½ oz) cartons of fruit or flavoured yoghurt

Lightly whip the cream. Gradually add the condensed milk while you continue to whip. When all the milk has been added, fold in the yoghurt with a spatula. Freeze for at least 4 hours in an airtight container.

Yvonne's Malva Pudding

Yvonne is a very good friend of mine who lives in Cape Town. I used to teach her daughter to play the harp and whenever I gave concerts Yvonne would present me with a cookbook instead of a bouquet of flowers. She is the most fantastic cook and we used to swap recipes long before I ever thought of writing cookbooks myself.

Makes 8 portions

Sponge pudding
225 g (8 oz) sifted flour
1 egg, lightly beaten
1½ teaspoons bicarbonate of soda
5 ml (1 tsp) vinegar
100 g (4 oz) caster sugar
250 ml (8 fl oz) milk
a pinch of salt
1 heaped tablespoon apricot jam
15 g (½ oz) butter

Sauce
175 g (6 oz) caster sugar
250 ml (8 fl oz) milk
250 ml (8 fl oz) whipping or double cream
25 g (1 oz) butter
5 ml (1 tsp) vanilla essence

Pre-heat the oven to 180°C/350°F/Gas 4 and grease an oven-proof dish that measures approximately 25 x 20 cm (10 x 8 in). Combine the ingredients for the pudding to form a smooth batter. Pour into the prepared dish and bake for 35 minutes or until a knife comes out clean. Combine all the ingredients for the sauce in a pan, stir over a medium heat, bring to boiling point but do not boil. Make several holes in the top of the pudding with a skewer and then pour half the sauce into them and serve. Serve the remaining sauce on the side.

Nicholas's Dream Dessert

My son Nicholas and I concocted this heavenly dessert together. We decided to design a pudding around it using fresh summer berries, cream and crushed meringue. The pudding was a huge success with the whole family and there was not a scrap left. This is also an easy and fun recipe to make with your child. (*See photograph opposite*)

Makes 6 portions

450 g (1 lb) raspberries
3-4 tablespoons icing sugar
175 g (6 oz) strawberries, hulled and cut into quarters

300 ml (½ pint) whipping cream
a few drops vanilla essence
4 ready-made meringues (about 75 g/3 oz)

Put the raspberries into a saucepan and heat gently until they become mushy. Press the raspberries through a sieve and reserve the sauce in a small saucepan. Add the sugar to taste and stir over a low heat until the sugar is dissolved. Stir the remaining raspberries and strawberries into the sauce.

Whip the cream together with the vanilla essence until stiff but not too thick. Break the meringues into pieces and fold these into the whipped cream. Spoon a little of the cream and meringue mixture into each of the glasses, cover with some of the berries and then repeat each layer and top with a sprig of mint or some crushed meringue.

Berried Treasure

The fruits turn a wonderful rich dark red colour, which children love, and this is a good recipe for using up fruits that aren't particularly sweet. Don't worry if you don't have all the fruits listed below.

Makes 6 portions

2 peaches
6 plums or apricots
100 g (4 oz) strawberries
100 g (4 oz) blackberries

100 g (4 oz) blueberries
100 g (4 oz) cherries
40 g (1½ oz) sugar
100 g (4 oz) raspberries

Halve and stone the peaches, and cut each half into four. Halve and stone the plums or apricots and cut each half in two. Put all the fruits except the raspberries into a heavy-bottomed saucepan, sprinkle over the sugar and simmer for 10–12 minutes. Add the raspberries last as they tend to become mushy, and simmer for 2–3 minutes. Serve cold or hot with vanilla ice cream.

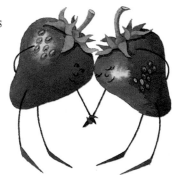

Index

almonds:
  and poppy seed cake, 169
  ice cream, 176
amaretto biscuits, with summer fruit
  brulee, 176
Annabel's 15-minute tomato sauce, 64
Annabel's apricot cookies, 160
Annabel's no-bake train cake, 164
Annabel's tasty chicken skewers, 81
antioxidants, 133
apples:
  and blackberry pudding, 177
  and carrot muffins, 36
  and courgette chicken burgers, 92
  and plum crumble, 184
  and sultana cake, 163
  smiles, 170
apricots:
  and coconut muffins, 160
  cookies, 160
Auntie Ruthie's quick and easy
  cheesecake, 180

bagel snake, 58
baked marrow with cheesy topping, 132
baked potatoes, 136, 137
bananas:
  and chocolate pancakes, 182
  and strawberry yoghurt shake, 30
  bread, best-ever, 31
  cake, 158
basket-weave chicken breasts. 90
beansprouts with noodles and prawns,
  128
beef:
  marinated with vegetables, 104
  skewers, 106
berried treasure, 186

best-ever banana bread, 31
best-ever oatmeal raisin cookies, 169
biscuits:
  apricot, 160
  coconut kisses, 165
blackberry and apple pudding, 177
boiled eggs, 29
Bolognese sauce, 68
  turkey, 74
bread, 28
  cheesy shapes, 32
breakfast cereals, 28
breakfast cereal plus, 29
breakfast recipes, 26-39
breakfasts, quick ideas, 29
brown rice 'risotto', 148
brownies, glossy dark and white
  chocolate, 172
burgers:
  barbecued, 86
  chicken, 92
  mini, 99
  turkey, 86
  vegetable, 143
buzzy bees, 52

cakes:
  almond and poppy seed, 169
  banana, 158
  carrot, 154
  chocolate chip, 159
  fairy, 156
  strawberry cream, 168
  sultana and apple, 163
  train, 164
  walnut and coffee, 162
calcium, 22
caramelised almond ice cream, 176

caramelised onion and Gruyère tart,
  142
carbohydrates, 19
carrots:
  apple and muffins, 36
  cake, 154
  gratin of, 141
  with mashed potato, 143
cheese:
  and tomato lasagne, 69
  bread shapes, 32
  chive and tomato omelette, 34
  pretzels, 60
  topping, 132
cheesecake, 180
chicken:
  and potato pancake, 88
  balls in sweet and sour sauce, 80
  breasts, basket-weave, 90
  burgers with courgette and apple, 92
  creamy with vegetables, 84
  curried, 88
  drumsticks, 89
  piccata, 84
  rissoles, 94
  Sasha's, 80
  skewers, Annabel's 81
  teriyaki, 81
  with penne, tomatoes and basil, 73
  yakitori, 94
Chinese noodles with prawns and
  beansprouts, 128
Chinese-style mince with noodles, 102
chocolate banana pancakes with toffee
  sauce, 182
chocolate chips:
  and raspberry muffins, 154
  cake, 159

coconut:
  and apricot muffins, 160
  kisses, 165
coffee and walnut gâteau, 162
cookies:
  apricot, 160
  oatmeal raisin, 169
courgette:
  and apple chicken burgers, 92
  fritters, 138
  gratin, 138
creamy chicken with vegetables, 84
crumble, apple and plum, 184
cucumber crocodile, 48
curry, chicken, 88

delicious vegetable rissoles, 146
Denise's easy spinach pie, 133
desert island pineapple, 178
desserts, 176-87
diet, choosing a healthy, 21
dressing for dinner, 55
dried fruit compotes, 29
dried herbs, 8
drop scones, lemon and raisin, 38
dry foods, 8

easy Bolognese sauce, 68
easy yakitori chicken, 94
eggs:
  and children, 28
  boiled, 29
  scrambled, 29
  see also omelettes
Eyelyn's lokshen pudding, 184
Evelyn's tasty fish pie, 126

fairy cakes, funny face, 156

fat in foods, 19
finger licking chicken drumsticks, 89
fish:
  fingers, 122
  pie, 126
  recipes, 110-129
fishing for compliments, 120
fluffy baked potatoes, 137
food labels, reading, 24
food pyramid, 18
forest fruit lollies, 178
freezer, stocking, 9
freezing cooked foots, 24
French toast, 35
  funny shape, 29
fried rice, 132
fritters, courgette, 138
frozen yoghurt ice cream, 185
fruit:
  brulée, 176
  curried chicken, 88
  dark chocolate bars, 170
  for breakfast, 28
  homemade muesli, 38
  in diet, 20
  juice, 28
  milkshakes, 29
  salad with honey yoghurt dressing, 29
  stewed, 29
funny face fairy cakes, 156

glossy dark and white chocolate brownies,
  172
good old-fashioned chicken soup, 47
grains, 28
gratins:
  of carrots, 141
  of courgette, 138

ground spices, 8
Gruyère and onion tart, 142

healthy diet, choosing, 21
heavenly barbecued burgers, 86
honeyed lamb cutlets, 102

ice cream:
  almond, 176
  frozen yoghurt, 185
ice lollies, forest fruit, 178
individual pinwheel pizzas, 50
iron, 22

Japanese salad dressing, 55
Josie's delicious carrot cake, 154

king prawn stir-fry, 114

lamb:
  cutlets, 102
  leg of, 103
  luscious, 106
Lara's lasagne, 64
Lara's lovely onion soup, 44
lasagne, 64
  with spinach, cheese and tomato, 69
leek and watercress soup, 46
lemon and raisin drop scones, 38
lentil soup, 45
linguine with spring vegetables, 70
Lloyd's leg of lamb, 103
Louise's apple and blackberry pudding, 177
lunchbox ideas, 43, 48-61
  balanced, 60

macaroni cheese, 68
mackerel fillets, 113

Maria's luscious lamb, 106
marinading, 104
marinated beef:
  skewers, 106
  with vegetables, 104
marrow, baked, 132
Mars bar and rice crispies slice, 172
mashed potato with carrot, 143
meal planners, 10-17
meat recipes, 96-109
meatballs:
  with tomato sauce, 98
  turkey, 85
Mediterranean tomato soup, 48
mermaid morsels, 116
milk:
  smuggling extra, 22
  milkshakes, fruity, 29
mince meat, Chinese-style, 102
mini baked potatoes, 137
mini burgers with cheese stars, 99
mini meatballs with tomato sauce, 98
mousse, raspberry, 177
muesli:
  fruity homemade, 38
  with yoghurt, honey and fruit, 30
muffins:
  apple and carrot, 36
  apricot and coconut, 160
  chocolate chip and raspberry, 154
  savoury, 36
Mummy's minestrone, 46

nasi goreng, 93
Nathalie's chocolate chip cake, 159
Nicholas's dream dessert, 186
noodles with beansprouts and prawns, 128
nourishing lentil soup, 45
nuts, 28
  and allergies, 25

oatmeal raisin cookies, 169
oils, 9
omelettes:
  cheese, chive and tomato, 34
  ratatouille, 146
onions:
  and Gruyère tart, 142
  soup, 44
  sauce, 116
Orient express, 66
oyster sauce and vegetables, 148

packed lunches, 42
paella, 123
pancakes, 35
  chocolate banana, 182
pasta sauce, quick and easy, 76
pasta:
  bow-tie with peas and proscuitto, 72
  Scarlett's, 76
  simple, 65
  penne with chicken, tomatoes and basil,
  73
  tagliatelle with prawns and vegetables,
  75
  tuna, 127
  vegetable, 74

perfect baked potatoes, 136
perfect Chinese fried rice, 132
perfect paella, 123
perfect pancakes, 35
Peter's Jamaican patties, 107
pineapple, desert island, 178
pizzas, 50
  ciabatta, 52
  spotted snake, 150
plum and apple crumble, 184
poppy seed and almond cake, 169
porridge, 30

posh fish fingers, 122
potatoes:
  baked, 136
  leek and watercress soup, 46
  mashed with carrot, 143
poultry recipes, 78-95
prawns:
  stir-fry, 112
  with Chinese noodles and beansprouts,
  128
  with tagliatelle and vegetables, 75
pretzels, cheesy, 60
protein, 19
  for breakfast, 28

quick ciabatta pizza, 51

raisin, lemon and drop scones, 38
raspberries:
  and white chocolate chip muffins, 155
  mousse, 177
ratatouille omelette, 146
refrigerator, stocking, 9
rice crispies slice, 172
risotto:
  brown rice, 148
  summer, 134
  tomato and basil, 149
rissoles:
  chicken, 94
  vegetable, 146

salad bar, 54
salad dressings:
  dressing for dinner, 55
  Japanese dressing, 55
  soy sauce, 54
salmon fillets in a watercress sauce, 122
salmon teriyaki, 118
salt, in diet, 21

sandwiches, 42
  double-decker, 42
  fillings, 43
  novelty-shaped, 58
  pinwheel, 42
Sasha's chicken, 80
sauces, 8
  Bolognese, 68
  orange, 116
  pasta, 76
  soy dressing, 54
  sweet and sour, 80
  toffee, 182
  tomato, 64, 85, 98
  watercress, 122
savoury muffins, 36
Scarlett's pasta, 76
seasonings, 9
seeds, 28
shepherd's pie, 108
Simon's Multi-layered shepherd's pie,
  108
Simon's simple pasta, 65
simply super salmon teriyaki, 118
snacks, 48-61
soups:
  chicken, 47
  lentil, 45
  minestrone, 46
  onion, 44
  potato, leek and watercress, 46
  tomato, 48
  vegetable, 45
soupa tuna tagliatelle, 127
soy sauce dressing, 54
spaghetti Marinara, 117
spinach:
  lasagne, 69
  pie, 133
spotted snake pizza, 150

spring rolls, vegetarian, 140
stewed fruit, 29
stir-fries, 64
  king prawn, 114
  prawn, 112
storecupboard, contents of, 8-9
strawberries:
  and banana yoghurt shake, 30
  cream cake, 168
sugar in foods, 19
  and tooth decay, 159
sultana and apple cake, 163
summer fruit brulee, 176
summer risotto, 134
super vegetarian spring rolls, 140
sweet and sour sauce, 80
swirly porridge, 30

tagliatelle:
  tuna, 127
  vegetable, 74
  with prawns and vegetables, 75
tart, onion and Gruyère, 142
tasty and healthy vegetable soup, 45
tasty 10-minute prawn stir-fry, 112
teddy bear chicken rissoles, 94
teriyaki:
  chicken skewers, 81
  glazed mackerel fillets, 113
  salmon, 118
terrific turkey schnitzels, 92
three-cheese macaroni, 68
tinned produce, 8
tiramisu, 181
toffee sauce, 182
tomatoes:
  and basil risotto, 149
  and cheese lasagne, 69
  omelette, cheese and chive and, 34
  sauce, 64

with mini meatballs, 98
  with turkey, 85
  soup, 48
  with penne, chicken and basil, 73
train cake, 164
tuna tagliatelle, 127
turkey:
  Bolognese, 74
  burgers, 86
  meatballs with tomato sauce, 85
  schnitzels, 92

upside-down banana cake, 158

vegetables:
  burgers, 143
  in diet, 20
  soup, 45
  tagliatelle, 74
vegetarian diet, 25
vegetarian recipes, 130-51
very easy Florentine fillets, 112
very easy raspberry mousse, 177
vitamin content, preserving, 73
vitamins, 23

walnut and coffee gâteau, 162
watercress:
  sauce, 112
  soup, 46
Welsh rarebit, 34

yakitori chicken, 94
yoghurt:
  shake, 30
  ice cream, 185
yummy fish in orange sauce, 116
yummy vegetables in oyster sauce, 148
Yvonne's malva pudding, 185

Annabel Karmel

Annabel is a leading author on cooking for children and has written several international best-selling books on the subject, including *The Complete Baby and Toddler Meal Planner*, the definitive authoritative guide on feeding babies and toddlers. Now it's the turn for the whole family to enjoy Annabel's recipes.

Annabel is the mother of three children, Nicolas 11, Lara 9 and Scarlett 7, and as a busy working mother knows how hard it is to create meals that the whole family will like.

A trained Cordon Bleu cook, she has combined the results of her research into child nutrition and the successful feedback from her children's books with her knowledge and love of cooking to produce delicious quick and easy-to-prepare meals that the whole family can enjoy together.

Annabel writes for a wide range of magazines and newspapers and appears regularly on television.

Acknowledgments

I want to thank all the children and parents who have been 'guinea pigs' to the successes and failures of my culinary experiments. In particular my mother, Evelyn Etkind, who very seldom uses her own kitchen but has hosted many dinner parties by raiding the contents of my fridge after a day's recipe testing; and my children Nicholas, Lara and Scarlett, who alas now claim that they are too grown-up to be fed purées and have eaten their way through all the recipes in this book and enjoyed lending a hand in cooking some too. Also my husband, Simon, who will be pleased to sit down to dinner in peace without having me ask, 'Well, what do you think?' before being given the chance to swallow the first mouthful.

I would also like to thank Amelia Thorpe, Joanna Carreras, Emma Callery, Christine Carter, Alison Shackleton, Daniel Pangbourne, Harry Ormesher, Val Barrett, Tessa Evelegh, David Karmel, Jacqui Morley, Marina Magpoc, Letty Catada, Nadine Wickenden and Jane Hamilton.